TO
my Reverend Father
in ☧

FROM
one of the least of
the Brethren
Bob Bendick

Feast of the Holy Trinity   — 1966

Toward a More Excellent Ministry

We Rejoice with You

As the official Publishing House of the church which we serve and as the publisher of this 125th-anniversary volume, it is a genuine pleasure to place into your hands this complimentary copy of TOWARD A MORE EXCELLENT MINISTRY.

We rejoice and thank God that He has blessed our church with an institution for training pastors that is alive to its modern responsibilities and eager that excellence and spiritual soundness characterize and shape its human product.

It is a privilege for us to play a part in this educational process. We trust that many of the theological and Biblical reference tools and resources we make available for your personal library during your academic years, as well as the great variety of devotional, administrative, inspirational, and practical materials from our presses that you will be using throughout your future ministry, will help you grow into a true servant of the living Word.

In reality, we are bound together in a lifelong pursuit of that Excellence in which we live and move and have our being.

We also pray that the Lord of the church will continue to richly bless the training program of the St. Louis seminary, enabling it to send forth men like you, on fire for Christ, thoroughly equipped to be the kind of shepherds and leaders that God and this complex, demanding world require.

CONCORDIA PUBLISHING HOUSE

Presented Founders Day
Dec. 9, 1964

Toward a More Excellent Ministry

Editors, RICHARD R. CAEMMERER

ALFRED O. FUERBRINGER

Concordia Publishing House, Saint Louis, Missouri

Concordia Publishing House, St. Louis, Missouri

Concordia Publishing House Ltd., London, W. C. 1

Copyright 1964 by Concordia Publishing House

Library of Congress Catalog Card No. 64-24267

Manufactured in the United States of America

Foreword

December 9, 1964, is the 125th anniversary of the founding of Concordia Seminary, St. Louis, Mo. This book is one contribution to the observance of it. Another volume is planned to tell the story of the school in detail.

The purpose of these essays is to describe the meaning of the holy ministry, as a group of seminary teachers see it. Beyond the description is a higher purpose: that the people of the church may share the vision of what the ministry to God's people is, that they may be infected with a sense of the urgency of it and pass it on to their sons, and that they may realize what is going on in their name in a school which is very much their own.

President Fuerbringer and the undersigned share in the editing of these essays. We have sought to let each colleague speak in his own idiom. No formal attempt has been made to produce these papers by conference between members of seminary departments. It should be said, however, that the structure of the seminary faculty and the fine rapport in which its members stand toward one another make these papers a reflection of the concerns and labors of them all.

President Fuerbringer has been in his position since 1953, after serving 14 years in pastorates and 12 years as president of Concordia Teachers College, Seward, Nebr. His travels in the interest of ministerial training are worldwide.

Harry G. Coiner, professor of pastoral theology and religious education since 1955 and director of placement, has 13 years of pastoral experience, 4 in the active Army chaplaincy and many more in the reserve (lieutenant-colonel), and three years' service as Secretary of Parish Education of the Eastern District.

David S. Schuller, associate professor of homiletics and pastoral theology, entered the staff in 1955. In addition to parish experience he has rendered nationwide service as consultant in parish planning and has invested his doctorate in sociology directly into the strategy of the church.

Carl S. Meyer, professor of historical theology since 1954 and director of graduate studies since 1960, has experience as parish pastor, college professor, high school administrator, and research scholar. He is editor of the *Concordia Historical Institute Quarterly* and is preparing the anniversary historical volume.

Arthur C. Repp, professor of religious education since 1945 and academic dean since 1952, after 14 years in the pastorate, served as executive of Synod's Board of Parish Education for several years. He was chairman of the Curriculum Commission, which developed the revised program of pastoral training in Synod. He is president of the Concordia Historical Institute.

Martin H. Franzmann is chairman of the department of exegetical theology and has been professor of New Testament exegesis since 1946. He is widely known as writer and lecturer in his field and as a member of synodical commissions on doctrinal unity and theology, on which he has represented the church also overseas.

Herbert J. A. Bouman has been professor of systematic theology since 1954, after 22 years in the pastorate. He has likewise been active in synodical commissions on doctrine and in representing the church overseas. He is widely used as lecturer to conferences in his field of specialty, the Lutheran Symbols.

William J. Danker, after 11 years of service in the pastorate, became Synod's pioneer missionary in Japan. After seven years of leadership in this field he became professor of missions and director of missionary training at the Seminary, in 1956. He has also served as consultant to national boards and organizations.

Leonhard C. Wuerffel has been dean of students since 1948. Prior to this post he served in campus and parish pastorates for 12 years and as professor at Concordia Teachers College in Seward, Nebr. His massive experience and his doctorate are utilized in the field of student guidance.

George W. Hoyer has been professor of homiletics and liturgics since 1954, after an 11-year pastorate. A pioneer in the accent on worship which pervades the organized youth program of the church, he has been a valued resource for many organizations of the church. He is in wide demand as a preacher.

Martin H. Scharlemann has been professor of New Testament exegesis since 1952. He came from the Air Force chaplaincy, in which he still holds a reserve commission (colonel). Prior to this he had pastoral experience. From a scholar in several fields as well as a pastoral servant, his words of respect to the ministry have unique significance.

The editors express their appreciation to Concordia Publishing House and to the Rev. Roland Seboldt for their assistance in the preparation of this book.

RICHARD R. CAEMMERER

Contents

in enrollment. A second relocation to Clayton, Mo.,
marks the turn from the age of C. F. W. Walther and
Franz Pieper to the present time of swift change and
challenge.

CARL S. MEYER

In contrast to the "American plan" of ministerial education, Concordia Seminary requires a closely defined
pretheological training for entrance. These prerequisites,
and the program of training at the seminary itself, stand
in direct relation to the needs of the church, the pastor,
and the servant of the Word who functions in a special
ministry.

ARTHUR C. REPP

The basic function of training in the Scriptures is to help
the student and ultimately the pastor to listen to the
Word of God. The barriers for this listening are formidable. They are surmounted by arduous labor toward
competence in the Biblical languages and literature. This
effort brings high rewards for the pastor and his people.

MARTIN H. FRANZMANN

The Christian pastor is a minister of the Word. From
his seminary the Lutheran pastor should receive a distinctive approach to the Bible and its message. The point
of view toward the Bible and the Christian faith which
is given by the Lutheran Symbols is the perspective of
the Gospel. The pastor must be able to communicate this
perspective.

HERBERT J. A. BOUMAN

Concordia Seminary stresses missionary training because
the church has a mission to the world. All students take
basic mission courses. All incorporate the mission outlook in their work, whatever their destination. Many

Toward a More Excellent Ministry

Toward a More Excellent Ministry

ALFRED O. FUERBRINGER

As Concordia Seminary, St. Louis, Mo., marks the 125th anniversary of its founding in Altenburg, Perry County, Mo., in 1839, even a quick look at the five quarter centuries of its history is illuminating.

1839: The little log cabin "college" was built by three unemployed candidates for the holy ministry in a remote corner of what was then the Far West. Nevertheless, the new institution was boldly publicized in an effort to make it known and to attract students.

1864: By this time Concordia Seminary had been moved and was well established in St. Louis, at that time one of the most important cultural centers of the United States. The founders of the school were still in very vigorous years, as illustrated by their conduct and promotion of the school. They had excellent relationships with their community.

1889: The last members of the founding generation were passing from the scene. The seminary and its supporting Synod were beginning to move into a cultural isolation, although there was a great numerical expansion because of the large influx of German immigrants into the country.

1914: The second generation was in its prime, but at the beginning of World War I Concordia was a German seminary of a German church. It was not too well known even in St. Louis.

1939: At the celebration of the seminary's centennial few

sons of the founders were still alive. By the time World War II began, the language barrier, which had hemmed in the Missouri Synod, had crumbled.

1964: The third generation is still on the scene. The Missouri Synod, and Concordia Seminary with it, have been thrust in an increasing measure into the ecclesiastical limelight and will need to find their proper place and sphere of activity in this new situation.

It is our hope that the entire observance of the 125th anniversary of Concordia Seminary, and particularly the publication of this volume of essays, will glorify our God through the thanks and praise we offer to Him for His guidance and for the rich blessing unfailingly granted to the seminary for the many years of its existence. This booklet is also to serve as an expression of appreciation for the role of the membership of the entire Synod in the training of the many pastors who have studied at our school, for the interest it has taken in our work, and for the support it has given to the school. The graduating class of the current academic year raises the total number of men who have been given to the ministry of our Synod by Concordia Seminary to more than 7,500. They have been, and are, active in a variety of ministries: in parishes of all types, as faculty members of educational institutions (high schools, colleges, universities, seminaries), in campus ministries at hundreds of schools outside our own synodical system, in military, hospital, and other institutional chaplaincies, as district and synodical executives and leaders in various types of church-related organizations, as writers and editors of church publications and probably a number of other forms of ministry. While the total of nonclerical alumni is not very large, it does include a number of laymen who are highly dedicated and able workers in their local congregations, the Districts, and the Synod. Our alumni are found today

4

in all of the 50 united states, in about two dozen other countries, on every continent and in every climate.

While we are grateful for the large number of students that have come to us for their theological studies and have gone forth to serve in the ministry of the Gospel, our chief aim is, and must always be, to strive for excellence in our work and product. We do not seek this goal to foster pride or an attitude of superiority, but because, when it comes to the service of our Lord and His church, we dare not be satisfied with anything but the best that lies within our power. "Toward a more excellent ministry" is therefore not merely a slogan. It includes an admission of our inability to do the job as we ought, in fact, to do anything at all, without our Lord's guidance and help. It is also an expression of our confidence that He will bless our efforts to improve the quality of our work and our product. And finally it is the expression of our determination to put forth greater effort toward sending out into the church and the world the kind of ministers of the Gospel that are sorely needed.

Many types of service must be rendered by theologically educated servants of Christ. As a result much specialized training is under way at Concordia Seminary. Even before graduation nearly a score of men annually receive training and commissions as officers in Army or Navy reserve chaplaincies, nearly 50 have had extended experience in a psychiatric hospital as helpers and orderlies. Many have participated in campus ministries, others in work in the inner city, a few in foreign countries. The School for Graduate Studies provides special training for men continuing after graduation or returning, while in the pastorate, for advanced studies, available also for teachers and laymen qualified for, and interested in, theological studies. From this group come many of the teachers in the system of synodical schools for the education of future workers in the church.

5

This book does not say much about the specialization we offer but focuses on a fundamental program of training, that for the parish ministry. We find this to be a basic necessity, for no matter what the program of ultimate specialty may be, a factor which it has in common with all the rest must be the readiness and the skill to spend one's self for others, to be a servant of the Word, by which men are set free from sin and made and kept members of the body of Christ in the church.

As this booklet sets forth the story of Concordia Seminary, what it has become by the grace of God and what it is endeavoring to do with His help, we trust that it will be of service to the entire membership of our Synod, specifically to those who are active in recruiting future ministers as well as to the parents of children that are potential seminary students. One of the factors which has made the history of The Lutheran Church — Missouri Synod the exciting story it is and has at the same time provided one of the chief reasons for its wonderful growth is the fact that from the very time of the arrival of our immigrant ancestors in this country, they and their children and children's children were uniquely interested, not so much in higher education for its own sake as in a high caliber program of education for the ministries of the church. We trust that this level of interest will be sustained and that the years to come will see an even greater measure of gifts bestowed by our generous and loving God.

CONCORDIA — what a beautiful name! Our founding fathers without a doubt chose it to indicate both the content of the theological instruction to be given at the new school and the attitude which should pervade everything going on there. It was the first of many Concordias in this country. May it always be true to its name and a good example for others.

The Pastor in the Church

HARRY G. COINER

Who are the young men who receive diplomas from
Concordia Seminary and go out from the academic halls in St. Louis
with a call to serve people as ministers of the Gospel in many
parts of the world? They have come as members of Christian
congregations, men who have heard and obeyed the call from God
to give themselves to the public ministry in the church.[1] The
process began when they believed that Christ willed that the Gospel
should be preached and that the church should be cared for by
gifted men trained and called for this special task. On the heels
of this basic faith came the personal conviction that they had a call
from Christ to give themselves for this work. In most instances,
parents, teachers, and pastors encouraged them to begin the long
period of study and training necessary for the task. Through the
years their teachers and professors nurtured and guided them in
their studies and personal life. The pastors where they vicared
helped them get the feel of the ministry as they were guided and
corrected in their first steps toward serving people pastorally. At
last, eight years beyond high school, the eventful day of graduation
and assignment sends them out to take their places in the long
line of ordained clergy who are giving their lives to the work of
feeding and leading God's people.

9

Who Is This Man, the Pastor?

Who is this man, then, the minister dressed in the conservative clothing, maybe wearing a clerical collar, who is called "pastor" by his people? What is his job in the church? He is certainly more than an angelic "fuddy-duddy," a good fellow who preaches on Sundays and studies his sermons and visits his people during the rest of the week. People often have different views of the pastor's role in the church. Sometimes he is the "preacher," the man in the pulpit. Sometimes he is the man who manages the church, a person who coordinates and supervises the spiritual activities of the people in a church program. Sometimes he is seen as one who helps the members of the church at their Christian work, the big brother who helps all the little brothers as he counsels and directs them in the things of the Christian faith and life.

Although all these views are partly true, none is entirely complete. Biblical history and doctrine give us the truer image of the pastor's task. The activity of mediating God to people runs through the history of God's dealing with men. God's people have always had some person among them to speak about God to them, to shepherd them, and to lead and rule them in terms of the Word of God to men. God gave leaders like Moses, prophets like Isaiah, priests like Aaron, and rulers like David. These men were servants of God to men whose service or ministry pointed to the one great Servant, Jesus Christ, who "came not to be ministered unto but to minister and to give His life a ransom for many" (Matt. 20:28). The line of the ministry of the old covenant runs to Jesus Christ and through Him into the ministry of the New Testament church. It was His will that repentance and remission of sins should be preached in His name among all nations (Luke 24:47). This task He gave His church when He told the disciples, "As My Father hath sent Me, even so send I you. . . . Whosesoever sins ye remit, they are remitted unto them; and whosesoever sins ye retain, they are retained." (John 20:21-23)

The Church Shares
in the Mission of Christ

With the coming of Christ what all the ages had desired to see and hear moved into the human scene. He announced the decisive redeeming act of God and performed it (Luke 10:23, 24). He announced that the kingdom of God had come into the world, and He summoned men into that kingdom. He called His disciples to be the nucleus of a new Israel and assured them that "it is your Father's good pleasure to give you the Kingdom" (Luke 12:32). All that Christ has and will give to men becomes the possession of the people of God — but for a reason. "You are a chosen race, a royal priesthood, a holy nation, God's own people, that you may declare the wonderful deeds of Him who called you out of darkness into His marvelous light" (1 Peter 2:9). All Christians are members of a priesthood who bring their sacrifice of prayer and self-consecration (1 Peter 2:5). All are called to love one another and serve one another (John 13 and 15; Rom. 12 and 13). All are to sustain one another through common sharing of God's grace and so edify one another toward the maturity that they are to have in Christ. The responsibility which each member has toward fellowship and mutual care is activated by the Word of God as it is spoken to people and conveyed to them in the sacraments with the final goal in view — the one great body in Christ (Eph. 5:1-16; Rom. 12:1-21; 1 Cor. 12; Col. 3:1-17). The purpose of all love and service in the church is that the life of Christ is conveyed constantly to those who have it, to those who falter, and to those who have not had it at all. (Matt. 18; Gal. 6:1-10; Matt. 28:20)

11

The Church's Life Is Ministry

The church is apostolic in its essential nature because it shares in the mission of the Son by the Father and is empowered by the Holy Spirit (John 20:21-23).[2] God is working out His purposes in the world when He calls Christians to a life of service or ministry, giving each believer a spiritual gift which is to be received and employed for the common good. Life in the church involves some form of ministry *(diakonia)*.[3]

In the first place, God is at work within the body of the Christian fellowship through the ministry of Word and Sacraments bringing His people to life and keeping them alive with the life of the Spirit and giving them the life of Christ to share with one another (Eph. 4). In the second place, God is at work in the believers within the body of the Christian fellowship motivating and directing their ministry to one another in faith and love in all situations and relationships of life as they share in the confession of their faith and in their witness of the redemptive act of God (1 John 1:3-7; 1 Cor. 7; Heb. 10:16-25). In the third place, God is at work in His church directing the ministry of the believers toward others who do not have the life of God (2 Cor. 5:17-19; 1 Peter 2:9, 10). They are to call out to the world, "Be reconciled to God [He has sent redemption] and take your place in the reconciled community [you have been redeemed]."

Christ, church, ministry — these are New Testament realities which go together and result in the activities of God's calling, upbuilding, and sending: in God's people responding, edifying one another, and going out. The church derives its ministry from Christ. It is the community in and through which God accomplishes His will and works out His redemptive purposes in the world through Jesus Christ. God's people are loyal to Him and trust in Him, and in faith they offer themselves to God that He may use their service and sacrifice. They exist not for themselves but for God and His world. (Eph. 3:9-11)

God Established a Special Ministry

In order that through His church Christ may be made manifest to the world which He died to save, the nature of the relationship between the members of the church and God through Christ and of the members of the church with one another in Christ is vital. Therefore Christ has given His church a special ministry in the sense of certain persons set apart to perform certain essential functions within the fellowship, so that the church may worship God in thankful remembrance of His saving act in Christ and may witness for Him to the world.

The apostles were called by Christ directly. Later the church called men whom Christ had gifted and ordained them with the laying on of hands to function as Christ's undershepherds to feed and lead the church on His behalf and according to His direction. The church believes that God uses the holy ministry as a primary means of getting His life-giving and life-keeping Word to men.[4] For this reason, the holy ministry as an office or function is God's ordinance for the church and is essential to the life of the church. It is, therefore, no mere prudential arrangement. The persons called to the public ministry are Christians and members of the church like all the rest — but by their call, both from Christ and the church, they are set apart to bear a pastoral concern for all. Like the apostles, pastors render a special service to the church. They are agents and workmen of God (2 Cor. 4:1, 2; 2 Tim. 2:24) and servants of God's people. (2 Cor. 4:5)

The Lutheran Confessions gratefully recognize that the ministry of Word and Sacraments is a gift of God to the church and name this ministry as the highest office or function in the church, noting that the chief service in the church is to teach the

Gospel.[5] Churches are not to despise the gifts bestowed for their life and well-being, but are duty bound before God, according to divine Law, to ordain for themselves pastors and ministers.[6] "The ministry of the Word has God's command and glorious promises . . . for the church has the command to appoint ministers; to this we must subscribe wholeheartedly, for we know that God approves this ministry and is present in it [that God will preach and work through men and those who have been chosen by men]." [7]

The Pastor Is
God's Gift to the Church

The pastor is a person given to God's people, a gift of Christ to the church. In Eph. 4 the apostle begs the Christians to lead a life worthy of the calling to which they are called, and to forbear (support) one another in love in order to maintain the unity of their common life together. That they might be able to serve and support one another and accomplish God's planned good, grace was given to each one according to the measure of Christ's gift. And His gifts were varied, but given to a specific end. "And these were His gifts: Some to be apostles, some prophets, some evangelists, some pastors and teachers, to equip God's people for work in His service, to the building up of the body of Christ." (Eph. 4:11, 12 NEB)

We see, then, that Christ has given certain persons to the church to equip the members themselves for the work of ministry.[8] Luther chose to say in his translation of the New Testament: "dass die Heiligen zugerichtet werden zum Werk des Amts." The pastoral ministry is God's means in His church by which His people are equipped to do the work He planned for them to do; it is a holy means by which His people are activated and directed to the target

14

of unity and maturity and service. God has devised and ordained a ministry through which the life of Christ flows from the Head into the body as a whole.

Believing that the ministry of Word and Sacraments is essential and not merely accidental to the life of the church, God's people "functionalize" this ministry and ordain (or install) men whom they call to feed and lead them, that is, preach and teach God's Word and guide their spiritual life of worship, witness, study, learning, and service. As church and ministry go together, so also the ministry of pastor and people will coincide. The ordained servant of the Word is properly a minister to ministers. The pastor serves the people when he enlists, trains, stimulates, and employs them in the essential tasks of the church. The emphasis is on mutuality of calling and service. The relationship between the ordained minister and the other members in the church is not one of relative rank or position in a hierarchy of status, but one of service and function (Luke 22:24-27). All are called, but all are not called to the same office or responsibility. Yet God has given the church a variety of gifts and a variety of functions for the common good (1 Cor. 12:4-11, 27-31). These gifts are to be employed to get the life of God started in people through the Gospel and to keep it going by the same Gospel. Some are gifted to guide and direct the activities and operations by which the building up and growth of the body goes on; others are able to lead the people in the church to do specific things in specific ways and sometimes at specific times.

The Public Ministry Serves
the Church in Various Ways

We ought to note that the Scriptures give various names to the persons who filled the offices of the public ministry in the

15

New Testament, and these names or titles were descriptive of their various functions. For example, as they had oversight of Christ's flock, they were termed bishops. As they fed the people with spiritual food, they were termed pastors. As they served Christ and His people in the church, they were termed ministers. As it was their duty to be grave and prudent, examples to the flock, and good governors of the household of God, they were termed presbyters or elders. As they were sent to declare the will of God to sinners and to beseech them to be reconciled to God through Christ, they were termed evangelists. As they dispensed the manifold grace of God through the administration of the sacraments according to the institution of Christ, they were termed stewards of the mysteries of God.

In our church and in our day the term "pastor" covers all these functions. When a person is called to serve as a pastor in the church, it belongs to his specific duties to pray to God for and with his people; to feed them by the reading, expounding, teaching and preaching of the Word of God; to cultivate in the congregation the activities of worship; to administer the sacraments; to instruct the children and youth and adults and to lead in the educational activity of the church; to visit and care for the people entrusted to him; to give special attention to the poor, the sick, the afflicted, and the dying; to be active as a missionary to those who are outside the church and to enlist his people in the same enterprise; to admonish the weak and reprove the erring; and with the appointed officers of the congregation to oversee the needs and tasks of the church and exercise the joint power of government.

When a minister is called to be a teacher in a theological seminary; or is given the task of an instructor of youth assembled in school, college, or university; or is appointed as a chaplain in an institution or the military forces; or in serving in other specific tasks which are appropriate to the ministry, he will take the pastoral oversight of those committed to his charge and be diligent to edify them with the Word of God.

When a minister is called to the work of a missionary or evangelist, he will do his work as a servant of Christ and exercise such powers as are given him in his call by those who have the right to call him.

When a minister is called to labor in the administrative work of the church, or to be a writer or editor, or to perform similar needful work, he will make full proof of his ministry by guiding and directing the church in the work of the Gospel and by disseminating the Gospel for the edification of the church.

The Personal Qualities
of the Pastor

The New Testament is careful to describe the qualifications of a man who fills the office of pastor. St. Paul tells Timothy not to be "hasty in the laying on of hands," that is, do not ordain a man to the ministry without serious consideration (1 Tim. 5:22). The man ordained to the office of the public ministry must be a tested, approved Christian, no novice in the faith, one whose ministry makes it apparent that he draws his strength from God (1 Tim. 5:22; 3:6; 4:5; 2 Cor. 6:3; 1 Cor. 9:24-27; 2 Cor. 3:4-6). His function must be manifestly the gift of the Holy Spirit. (1 Cor. 12:3-8)

The will to serve should be the first basic equipment the pastor has. Faithfulness in service is his very next requirement (Matt. 20:27; 1 Cor. 4:2). He must overcome any reliance on personal power over people or use of prestige to achieve his ends (1 Peter 5:1-4; Matt. 20:20-28). He must successfully battle the temptation to be in the job for what he can get out of it (1 Tim. 6:3-15). His personal life should be beyond reproach. (1 Tim. 3:7)

17

The servant of the Lord is to be a teacher and have the aptitudes for such teaching. That is to say, he is not to be contentious, but skilled in applying the Word of God to people in the church and outside. He is to be moderate, gentlemanly, relying for the effectiveness of his labors upon God and the Word of God rather than upon the skill of human debate (2 Tim. 2:24-26). He is to be equipped in sound doctrine and know how to handle Law and Gospel as a skilled workman. (1 Tim. 3:2; 4:16; 2 Tim. 2:14-16)

The term "pastor" implies competence and readiness, not at browbeating and prodding, but at feeding and leading the people to grow through the Word of life, including the members of his own family. His integrity resides in his personal life of faith and his Christian behavior toward the people he serves (Titus 1:6-11; 1 Tim. 3:2-12). He achieves his ends not by exercising his personal power or charm over people, nor does he stoop to dubious manipulations, but he relies totally on the Word of God (1 Peter 5:2-4; Acts 20:28).[9] In his preaching of the Word of God the pastor must be bold to speak and be free from concerns about the attitudes of men. (Acts 4:13; 9:29; 14:3; 19:8; 2 Cor. 5:18-20; 7:4)

From among God's people, one is chosen whose faith and life is the most stable to serve all the rest. The pastor in his life and witness is to be the "constant" in the church, one from whom the Word of God comes strong and pure, one whose life is an example to all. There is a great deal of ambiguity and incompleteness in living out the Christian faith, a great deal of weakness and sin. The pastor should exemplify the continuity of the Gospel at work in the life of a person whose life touches all the rest as he feeds and leads them to maturity of faith and service. (Titus 1:5, 6; 1 Peter 5:3)

18

The Ordained Ministry
Is God's Arrangement

A special ministry in the church was instituted with the calling of the apostles. They were commissioned by our Lord and sent to gather and edify congregations. The Scriptures tell us that the believers in the New Testament church selected, called, and ordained ministers.[10]

In the Lutheran Confessions the authority of the spiritual office is specifically defined by the words of Jesus, "He who hears you hears Me" (Luke 10:16). Consistently the confessions refer the commands and promises which Christ gave to the apostles to the public ministry through which in our time the Gospel is to be preached in the midst of the congregation and before all the world. The "glorious promises" which the ministry "has" are also acknowledged in the confessions by means of the apostolic and prophetic Word (Rom. 1:16: "The Gospel is the power of God for salvation to everyone who has faith"; likewise, Is. 55:11: "My Word that goes forth from My mouth shall not return to Me empty, but it shall accomplish that which I purpose").[11] The Lutheran Confessions summarize the meaning of Eph. 4:8 — "When He ascended on high He led a host of captives, and He gave gifts to men" — to say: "This authority to call, elect, and ordain ministers is a gift which no human power can wrest from the church." [12]

Through the office of the public ministry of Word and Sacraments God gives people justifying faith, establishes His church, and enables people to serve Him. God wills to preach and be active through men and those who have been chosen by men.[13] Therefore the Lutheran Confessions say that where the church is, there is also the ministry, and where there is preaching of the Gospel and the administration of the sacraments in accordance with the Gospel of Christ, there the church is also.[14]

19

Having been entrusted with the Gospel, the church has the commission to call men to "minister" it.[15] Believers are enjoined to honor their ministers, obey them and hear them, not merely because they speak for God but because God speaks through them what men must hear and believe.[16] When our ministers "teach, introduce, or institute anything contrary to the Gospel, we have God's command not to be obedient in such cases."[17]

The office of the public ministry is not determined from the standpoint of the person of the minister but always from the given of the divine institution of Christ. The words and deeds performed in the office do not receive their quality from the person — for example, from the fact that the minister is a Christian — but only from the action of God, who will work what He wills even through His enemies.[18] Yet the church is to be careful to call "suitable persons" and not "crude asses" (as the confessions remind us), but men of good repute, full of the Spirit and of wisdom.[19]

The public ministry is not a function which the church arranges, nor is it demanded by the moral principle of order (though order there should be, 1 Cor. 14:40), but it is an immediate institution of God through the command and promise of Jesus Christ. It has been said that the public ministry grows out of the royal priesthood of all believers and that it comes into being through the enabling commission of the congregation. This is not always understood. It is true that the pastor is a member of the priesthood and that he is commissioned by the congregation, but this does not mean that the authority of the pastor is the authority of the congregation transferred to one of its members. The idea of a transfer of the rights of the priesthood to the person of the pastor is foreign to the Lutheran Confessions.[20] The church may *confer* (in the sense of grant or bestow) its task of preaching the Gospel and administering the sacraments on one whom they call

20

and ordain in the name of Christ, but this task they do not *transfer* (in the sense of giving right or title to) to individuals in its membership. Rather the church *fills* this office entrusted to it by God and calls into this office instituted by God. In this office the pastor acts in the name and at the direction of God and in the stead of Jesus Christ. The called servant of the Word acts with authority given him not merely on the basis of an arrangement made by believers but on the basis of the divine institution and the authority of the Word of God.[21] Therefore the pastor does not exert his ministry by force but by the terms of the Word of God which he speaks and by the spiritual life which he fosters. By the same token the people are not passive, but respond to the pastor's ministry with their active participation in the Gospel as he calls them to church tasks and points out specifically what needs to be done and how to do it. The Lutheran Confessions strike off all authority in the church other than the Word of God and maintain that this authority is to be exercised through preaching, teaching, judging doctrine, counseling, advising, admonishing, etc.[22]

It is the duty of the church to be alert in recognizing that God has given this or that man the holy desire to serve in the office of the public ministry. When he is trained and ready to make the best use of his gifts, the church calls him to service and sets him apart by prayer and, according to ancient custom, the laying on of hands for the office of Word and Sacraments.

A capable and effective public ministry, under God, prospers the church and glorifies Jesus Christ. The church properly expends a great deal of its energy and concern toward training its pastors. Though the traditional roles of the pastor have changed in many ways, his task remains essentially the same. Yet the manner in which he must deploy both himself and the people he takes care of in order to set the cutting edge of the church against the world is worthy of thought, concern, and study both for himself and for those who train him for his role in the church. We look ahead now in the pages to come for a description of the ways and means employed by Concordia Seminary to train men for the holy ministry.

NOTES

1. Public ministry is so termed in the Lutheran Confessions as that office exercised *publice* — in behalf of the others, by their appointment. In this sense the public ministry of Word and Sacraments is distinguished from the personal ministry of love and service which all Christians render.

2. The apostolic nature of the church marks it as being sent to continue and participate in that movement of God toward man which began with the mission or sending of Christ and of the Holy Spirit (cf. Acts 13:4; 1 Peter 1:12). *A Theological Word Book of the Bible,* ed. Alan Richardson (New York: The Macmillan Co., 1951), p. 146.

3. The characteristic Greek word for "ministry" is *diakonia,* the favorite New Testament way of referring inclusively to the church's fundamental activity.

4. The term "holy" is properly connected to ministry because God commands it and promises to work through the men called to function in the ministration of Word and Sacraments.

5. Ap XV 42.

6. Treatise, Of the Power and Jurisdiction of Bishops, 72.

7. Ap XIII 12.

8. Alan Richardson, p. 148 says: "The apostles, prophets, etc., by *their* ministry prepare those to whom they minister to do their part in serving the whole body, and thus by the "ministry" or service of all, according to their vocation and grace (cf. Eph. 4:7), the body of Christ is built or grows to its full stature in Him (cf. Eph. 4:13-16)."

9. AC XXVIII 8.

10. For example, the case of Matthias in Acts 1:15-26 and Paul and Barnabas in Acts 13:1-3. At Miletus, St. Paul addressed the presbyters of Ephesus and said that the Holy Ghost had set them as overseers over the whole flock "too feed the church of God" (Acts 20:28). To aid the apostles in their work, or to supply their places in their absence, elders were ordained in every church in Acts 14:23 and Titus 1:5.

11. Cf. Ap XIII 11—14.

12. Treatise, Of the Power and Jurisdiction of Bishops, 67.

13. Ap XXVIII 18.

14. Ap VII and VIII 5.

15. "Wherever the church exists, the right to administer the Gospel also exists. Wherefore it is necessary for the church to retain the right of calling, electing, and ordaining ministers." (Treatise 67)

16. Ap XXVIII 18.

17. Acts 5:29; AC XXVIII 23.

18. Ap VII and VIII 3, 4.

19. Cf. Treatise 65; Ap XXVIII 3; Acts 6:3.

20. Edmund Schlink, *Theology of the Lutheran Confessions*, trans. Paul F. Koehneke and Herbert J. A. Bouman (Philadelphia: Muhlenberg Press, 1961), pp. 244—246.

21. Clear thinking about the unique office of the public ministry is helpful. This office is not the creation of the church, and it is given to the church not to please the church but to do the will of Christ. Therefore the pastor does not merely occupy his office as a member commissioned by the congregation; rather he stands over against the congregation as God's representative whom they have called and put in office by God's commission. At the same time, however, the public ministry is within the church and is not to be thought of as possessing any independent relation to Christ or any authority which is not given by Christ in the church and for the life and work of the church. Both pastor and congregation stand directly related to their Lord Jesus Christ under His Word. Thus neither the congregation nor the person of the pastor is the final authority, but the Lord, who governs both pastor and congregation through the Gospel and the sacraments.

22. AC V 1; XXVIII 5—11, 21; Ap XIII 7—13; XXVIII 13—16; Treatise 74.

BIBLIOGRAPHY

BOOKS

Caemmerer, Richard R. *Feeding and Leading.* St. Louis: Concordia Publishing House, 1962.

Foelber, E. E. "The Office of the Public Ministry," *Abiding Word.* Saint Louis: Concordia Publishing House, 1947. II, 474—492.

Fritz, John H. C. *Pastoral Theology.* St. Louis: Concordia Publishing House, 1932. Pp. 28—32.

Lueker, Erwin, ed. *Lutheran Cyclopedia.* St. Louis: Concordia Publishing House, 1954. See articles "Ministerial Office" and "Education of Ministry," pp. 686—692.

Schlink, Edmund. *Theology of the Lutheran Confessions.* Trans. by Paul F. Koehneke and Herbert J. A. Bouman. Philadelphia: Muhlenberg Press, 1961. Pp. 226—269.

23

Steege, M. J. "The Lutheran Pastor," *Abiding Word*. St. Louis: Concordia Publishing House, 1946. I, 389—409.

ARTICLES

Bartling, Walter J. "A Ministry to Ministers," *Concordia Theological Monthly*, XXXIII (June 1962), 325—336.

Caemmerer, Richard R. "The Universal Priesthood and the Pastor," *Concordia Theological Monthly*, XIX (August 1948), 561—582.

The Changing Target of the Pastorate

DAVID S. SCHULLER

The church and its ministry have been concerned about the rapid change sweeping through our American culture. For the most part writers within the church have documented these changes with a degree of alarm. They fear an erosion of standards, a secularization of values, breakdown within the family, a preoccupation with things. One Christian analyst reminds us that "plankton" is the microscopic form of vegetable life in the sea which drifts great distances as it is carried by the currents. He concludes: "Plankton is also an accurate term to describe the people of the 20th-century America. For we have lost our sense of direction; we seem powerless to direct our own destiny; we are without purpose in the world." [1]

To what extent are these charges true? Everyone senses to some extent the vastness of the changes in our material culture. Within a generation there has been a virtual revolution in the technological base of our culture. Labor-saving devices have shifted our earlier conceptions of units of human or animal power. Radical changes in refrigeration, transportation, building construction, mass media entertainment — all have affected daily life. And the changes are coming with even greater speed. It took a generation to double the number of automobile registrations; it took but seven years to triple the number of miles flown by planes; it took but half a decade to move television from an experimental curiosity to a household staple.

27

Of course these changes in the material base of our culture affected the patterns of our lives. But did they do more? Have we become "hollow men" whose inner life has "withered away"? Are we "men who have lost our souls"? To answer this question we must look at the changes which have taken place in our technology and ecology. But our greater concern is with the resultant changes among people.[2] How have these material changes affected our ideas and values, our social structures, and our patterns of behavior? Changes in the former may be theologically and ethically neutral; changes in the latter are obviously significant for the task of the church in its ministry to people.

I. EXTERNAL CHANGES:
DEMOGRAPHIC, TECHNOLOGICAL, ECOLOGICAL

Popular Growth. The first "given" with which the church must operate is the phenomenal explosion of population within the last half generation.[3] Many of the factors of contemporary life which we accept as "natural" are caused at least in part by the need to produce more diapers, cars, supermarkets, suburban developments, and churches for a U. S. population which will reach 235 to 240 million people within the next dozen years. The rate of increase remains so high that for several years the Census Bureau has been forced to continue to revise its projections upward. On the worldwide scene the annual net increase is 1.6 percent. Translated into individuals, this means an increase of 44 million more persons each year. Every time the hands on a clock indicate that one hour has passed, another 5,000 additional people are living on our globe. These are not possible projections for some distant future. They are descriptive of today. On the day on which these words are written the increase in population will be about 125,000.[4]

These raw increases in population must be interpreted

in terms of current history: the struggle of more people for self-determination, the emerging worldwide industrial society, the increased pressures upon older family patterns, the need for the rapid improvement and extension of public health programs, the need for meeting these new lives with the food, education, homes, and places of worship which they will need. It is obvious that while our society can handle the repercussions of the immediate increase in births with the joy of a growing industrial and agricultural system which thrives on expansion, this is not true for the under-developed countries of the world. Where the prospective increase will amount to some 180 percent — over against the United Nations' predictions of some 74 percent for more developed countries — this spells immediate tragedy and suffering in the form of sickness, starvation, and death.

We have become one world. Churches which would be true to their Lord in the next generation must lift their eyes beyond pressing parochial concerns. A staggering complex of problems and challenges will arise from the dimensions of population increases at home, but the problems and challenges abroad will be even greater.

The Rural Paradox. Another factor which the church must recognize in our day is a relatively high rate of personal mobility. As one looks to the distant past, one observes the migrations of peoples and clans. In the more recent past, stability remained the rule with a few individuals leaving their homeland for new opportunities across the ocean or in the city. But a pattern of individual and family mobility has become common in the past few years. For a half-decade the mobility rate has averaged about 20 percent a year. There is a great differential from one community to another. In some transitional slum communities the rate actually may rise to over 200 percent. In highly stable villages the rate may fall to 5 percent. But statistically the entire nation moves its residence in the course of five years. The church now must serve this shifting and mobile population.[5] In contrast to the past, people tend to be rootless and without a strong sense of permanence.

One of the strongest manifestations of this mobility has been seen in the heavy flow of people from the farms to the city. This pattern was established well before World War II. In the 15 years from 1920 to 1935, more than 46 million people moved from rural to urban communities. The war and postwar years have seen an acceleration of this movement. Beneath this change one uncovers a virtual revolution in rural America.

The basic definition of a farm has changed in recent years. One generation ago the average family farm in the Midwest consisted of 160 acres. This size was established generations before by the Homestead Act of 1862. These were family farms; often they operated just above the subsistence level. Land was cheap. Little equipment was used. Since family incomes were low, many rural young people decided to move to the city and seek their fortunes. World War II, with its heavy dislocations of young men, further aggravated the problem. Farmers were forced, then, to buy expensive new equipment to operate with fewer men. This in turn necessitated the purchase of more land to make the investment in equipment worthwhile.

The farm that confronts us today increasingly suggests a rural industry. The acreage is large; the land is expensive; the equipment is complex. A highly productive agricultural economy has resulted. A result of this change is that fewer farmers are producing more food. The total farm population continues to decline. In 1940 the total farm population amounted to 30 million. In the next 20 years it declined by one third. By 1965 the farm population will decrease to some 15 million people, approximately 8 percent of the nation.

This is a rural paradox. While there are fewer people in rural areas, the church has a major responsibility to minister to these people in these years of radical readjustment. Farmers need the church's resources to answer before God the question of their responsibility. Production will have to be increased in some areas to meet our growing population. Yet surpluses in other commodities present a vexing problem. What is Christian stewardship in a world of rich agricultural surpluses in our country, with malnutrition and starvation elsewhere? Further, a million and a half U. S. farm families are living on less than $1,000 a year. Economic decisions, the broader objectives of family living, soil and water conservation, the continued exodus of rural families, poverty among subsistence farmers, starvation abroad, the invasion of urban peoples into rurban areas, the relationship of the church to other rural institutions — these are some of the major ingredients of the challenge facing the rural ministry today.[6]

The Ailing Urban Giant. Cities continue to grow. Every U. S. census since the first in 1790 has shown an increased percentage of the population living in urban communities. At the end of the 18th century only 5 percent of the nation lived in cities; currently more than 65 percent of the population is urban. This change is reflected among our own church membership. At the close of 1961, 60 percent of our churches and mission stations were located in urban areas. Even more astounding, 77 percent of our members lived in urban communities.[7] The conception of the Missouri Synod as a rural church body is a fiction arising from a nostalgia for a simpler, more easily controlled past.

Cities are giants. They dominate the vital centers of power within the nation. From them the influences emanate to the rest of the land. Metropolitan areas are absorbing virtually all the population increase at the present time. Moreover, through unplanned and often unscrupulous land developments at the perimeters, metropolitan areas are consuming vital, rich truck-farming soil for the construction of more subdivisions, commercial developments, and industrial expansion. Size, density, heterogeneity — these are the three keywords which describe the uniqueness of cities.[8]

They remind the church that the challenge of the city is more profound than simply a ministry to a greater concentration of people. For cities change people. The city man begins to think differently; his values begin to change; he reacts to people on a different level; through urban pressures the core of his personality diminishes while the variations in his behavior patterns under various situations increase. More urban contacts are on the secondary level. People do not interact as total human beings. Their contacts are more segmental as each meets the other through the mask of the particular role which he plays in society. There is a greater degree of individuation and specialization in every segment of life from occupation to recreation. Sympathy and emotions become secondary to obligations and contractual relationships. A commercial economy triumphs; money becomes the least common denominator among people. A genuine sense of community is hard to develop; therefore people often seem less human, more rootless and frustrated.

Thus the urban giant is not well. Much of the heavy migration to the cities within the last 20 years has been of Negroes and poor Southern whites. In the last decade a number of large cities have experienced a high influx of Spanish-speaking Puerto Ricans. These peoples are attracted to the city by better economic, educational, and social conditions. Frequently rather abysmal slum conditions take the place of the heaven of which they dreamed. But even this is superior to the conditions which most of these families left. The city has not been able to adjust smoothly to the flood of these recent immigrants. The decade between 1950 and 1960 saw increases of between 25 and 150

32

percent in the nonwhite population in American cities. Los Angeles, Milwaukee, Dallas, Buffalo, and Denver all experienced more than a 90 percent increase in their nonwhite populations within the '50s.[9]

As a result pressure within the racial and ethnic ghettos increased. People were crowded and exploited. They had few salable skills. They were marginal to the surrounding culture. Their children were difficult to control as they grew away from their parents. Health and welfare problems increased. In fear and suspicion of this racial invasion the whites began to move to the suburbs by the hundreds of thousands. Often within two years an entire community changed from an exclusively white neighborhood into one almost entirely Negro or Puerto Rican. The whites took with them their institutions. Drugstores, funeral homes, insurance agencies — and churches — joined the mass exodus to the suburbs. Only the economic failures remained behind. Meanwhile hostilities, distrust, and suspicion grew among each group.

The church has a real target in the city. Two thousand years ago the Christian faith began its growth in the cities of Asia Minor. Today it faces the challenge of a new type of metropolitan culture which no civilization has yet known. The city in its people, its social structures and institutions, needs to hear the church speak a prophetic word of judgment upon its goals, values, and actions which exist apart from God. They also need to hear the priestly message of healing and love which the Gospel alone can bring to the brokenness and alienation that characterizes so much of modern life.[10]

The Exploding Suburbs. During the current 18-year period our national population is increasing by some 60 million. Forty million of these people will move into the suburban belts around our large cities. Eight of every 10 homes under construction are being built in suburbia. This new growth of suburbia as both a place and a way of life is another of the characteristics of our age to which the church must direct her attention.[11]

First, the church is concerned about the changes which may take place in a person's mental outlook in suburbia. Suburbia represents the end of the rainbow to millions of Americans. It is a place of lovely homes, large lawns, happy families — a haven of security and wealth. Those who live there quickly discover that there is no pot of gold at the end of this rainbow. Still the illusion lives on. Life there is likely to be rather insular. There is a striking homogeneity in any given development or community. People usually are of the same race, receive roughly the same income, are in the same age category, have children in about the same grade in school, have similar educational backgrounds and interests. The rich diversity which characterizes the city or village is gone. There are no very poor or very rich; usually there are no elderly or partial families. The zest and color which comes from living among people of varied backgrounds, races, and nationalities is absent. The need for witness and acts of love frequently becomes less sharp in such a setting.

While no one would suggest that suburbanites alone face the pressures of materialism, few would disagree that the problem arises in its most virulent forms there. For this segment of society the postwar prosperity has continued. Life is characterized by material abundance. Luxuries which were nonexistent a dozen years before have become family necessities. Comfort becomes the god most adored. Its chief high priests in advertising have created a worshipful public. Perhaps most significant of all is the speed with which one becomes accustomed to this higher level of living, gazing at the next step in consumption — confident that the American economic system will eventually provide it for him. The escalator moves only upward.

Churchmen have been perplexed in the presence of

suburbia. They fear that the church exists there in captivity, a domesticated institution which reflects the deeper values of the good life while pronouncing a gentle benediction upon the *status quo*. The church is popular and well supported. A few churchmen are optimistic. They see in suburbia the "beginnings of a new Christian era." All agree that the suburban church must confront its unique culture realistically and without embarrassment. The call to a genuine discipleship must be extended to suburbanites as well. "Religion in general" frequently is more foe than ally.[12] Suburbanites welcome the church as another organization to keep people active, busy, and moral. The haunting question is whether, with such a feeble introduction, the church can present God in the radical dimension of the Scriptures. Can people live in affluence and yet sense the total dependence of faith upon God alone? Today's suburban churches are forging the beginning of a positive answer to that challenge.

These vast changes have forced the church to reexamine its fundamental understanding of a parish or congregation. In the past people lived, slept, worked, and played in the same community. Today these functions are spatially separated. But the church continues to focus upon the area where people "sleep." For the average adult male the greater part of his life is lived away from the dormitory community which he calls home. "Home" usually implies the place where he spends his leisure time. Unwittingly the church in her patterns of parishes falls into this sphere of "leisure-time activity." She has continued to foster a pattern of organization which naturally appeals most heavily to those who remain where the church building is located, namely, to women and small children.

This forms one of the frontier questions: How should the church pattern itself in the next 25 years to reach out more effectively to all areas of life? In the past we have toyed with further improvement in the efficiency of our agencies. Now we seem to be developing the honesty and the courage to ask whether the basic pattern must be scrapped for a new model altogether.

II. INTERNAL CHANGES: VALUES AND BEHAVIOR

Population increases, the new role of leisure, the growth of metropolitan communities, the new importance of the smaller family unit, the growth of material culture — all these can be easily documented. But what of the man who lives in the midst of this culture? Which fact is the more significant: His basic continuity with the values and outlooks of his grandfather, or an increasing discontinuity?

The Post-Christian Era. The most perceptive thinkers of our day would answer "a basic discontinuity." Although they quibble about the most accurate words to describe the change, most agree that a fundamental change has taken place which might be termed a "post-Christian" age. One writer summarized the idea in the title of his book *The Death of God.*[13] These men are not denying God's existence, nor do they suggest that strong personal faith is no longer a viable option. They are writing from a cultural rather than a theological frame of reference. They suggest that Christianity has lost its position as a dominant and determining force in our age.

Without overidealizing an earlier age, in looking back one is impressed by a culture which found its center and meaning in a Christian interpretation of the universe. The thinking and understanding, the art and literature, the goals of life and the structures of society, found their significance and basic justification in God. Not every man was a Christian. But the assumptions which undergirded life included a sense of God and His place in the universe. Man as a created being ultimately was responsible to God. He had a basic nobility and grandeur in spite of the reality of sin.

These no longer are the undergirding presuppositions of our culture. Indeed an overtone of some of these concepts still is heard. But the former congruence between theology and culture is gone. The more perceptive poets and literary men sensed the change before the theologians did. Both Auden and T. S. Eliot express the same thought:

> We were always able to say: "We are children of God,
> And our Father has never forsaken His people."
> But then we were children. That was a moment ago,
> Before an outrageous novelty had been introduced
> Into our lives. . . .
> Just how, just when, It succeeded we shall never know:
> We can only say that now It is there and that nothing
> We learnt before It was there is of the slightest use,
> For nothing like It has happened before.[14]

In *The Rock* Eliot says:

> But it seems that something has happened that
>   has never happened before; though we know
>   not just when, or why, or how, or where.
> Men have left GOD not for other gods, they say,
>   but for no god; and this has never happened
>   before.[15]

Both men, deeply sympathetic to the Christian faith, are obsessed by the fundamental nature of this change. I think Eliot is right when he observes that the root difficulty is not the inability to *believe* certain things about God and people as our forebears did; the trouble is "the inability to *feel* towards God and man as they did." [16]

The Triumph of Secularism. This situation is culminating in the victory of secularism.[17] More areas of life are lived without direct reference to God or His will or purpose. It is secular in the sense of being autonomous. As one surveys the important segments of our culture — economics, politics, scientific investigation, higher education — one notes that virtually all of these have become secular. They can develop and find new directions and contents apart from any reference to the theological.

This is illustrated in our modern assumption that absolutes are unknowable. The average man will not deny the possibility of absolutes; to him the question is not relevant. For all practical purposes expediency becomes the rule: that which works is best. In areas where there are counterclaims which cannot be empirically verified — as in the claims of religions — one must adopt an attitude of tolerance.

But what of the church in the midst of this growing secularism? One might suspect that the current growth, vigor, and popularity of churches seriously questions this line of thought. Not at all. Sociologists such as Herberg have documented the parallel growth of religiosity and secularism in the last decade. "It is this secularism of a religious people, this religiousness in a secularistic framework, that constitutes the problem posed by the contemporary religious situation in America." [18] Bluntly stated, the increased vigor of institutionalized religion has done little to touch the real heart of secularism.

A British writer suggests a partial answer to our quandary in his term "perplexed Theists." [19] He pictures those within and outside the church as perplexed people because they cannot find it in their hearts to throw away the pieces of their belief, and yet they cannot accept the traditional structure. Their main concern is that in throwing away their religious beliefs they may at the same time throw away the necessary pieces of their civilization. Perhaps God is dead, but they fear they may still need Him. It is an uneasy secularism — but it is secular!

Relative Morality. This fundamental change in our values and outlook might be illustrated in the area of morality. An intense debate is being waged currently concerning the extent of the erosion of morality in our day. Juvenile behavior, honesty, political life, and sexual behavior are all used to indicate the fallen condition of public morals.

Without entering into this debate on the subject of morality today, two observations still must be made: First, one must acknowledge that every age has known its own manifestations of sin. It is true today that for an increased number of people sin is committed without a conscious awareness of wrongdoing in theological terms. Once when man sinned, he was fully aware of his transgression. Today's relative morality suggests to most people that as long as one does not seriously harm another, expediency is the chief standard of judgment. Secondly, men like Pittenger are correct when they suggest that we are dealing with the collapse of a widely held moral standard: "The fact is that the 'what you can get away with' idea is not so much the absence of *any* moral standard as it is the substitution of another idea of morality for the old one." [20]

But the new moral standard is so relative and flexible that to an earlier generation it appears to be nonexistent. Young people are deeply sensitive to the modes of conduct expected of them by their peers. To this code they adhere often with the zeal of an early Puritan. But on the broad front the code must "make sense" to them. If they do not acknowledge its validity, then that particular canon of morality simply does not exist for them. A basic pragmatism and laissez-faire attitude characterizes the "new" morality.

The target of the pastorate is indeed undergoing vast and rapid changes in these days. But the basic task remains the same. Man still is set as a creature into a world of order. God has made him for community; thus he must learn to live responsibly with other people. This basic pattern of community, however, has been disrupted by man's sin. In His Son God stepped decisively into human life to overcome our alienation and brokenness. He reaches out to people through the agency of His church to call men to life and to nurture them within its fellowship. As an institution the church lives under God's judgment and under His blessing. The pastor stands today at the vital center as he forges part of the answer to the query: "But when the Son of man comes, will He find faith on earth?"

NOTES

1. Robert A. Raines, *New Life in the Church* (New York: Harper and Brothers, 1961), p. 13.
2. David S. Schuller, "The Impact of American Culture on the Growing Child," *Lutheran Education,* IIIC, No. 3 (Nov. 1961), 99—109.
3. Richard M. Fagley, *The Population Explosion and Christian Responsibility* (New York: Oxford University Press, 1960).
4. Population Division, U. N. Department of Social Affairs, *The Future Growth of World Population* (New York: United Nations, 1958).
5. Carl A. Clark, *Rural Churches in Transition* (Nashville, Tenn.: Broadman Press, 1959).
6. Robert Larson, E. W. Mueller, and Emil Wendt, *Social Changes and Christian Responsibility in Town and Country* (Chicago: Town and Country Church, National Lutheran Council, 1960).
7. Bureau of Statistics, *1961 Statistical Yearbook of The Lutheran Church — Missouri Synod* (St. Louis: Concordia, 1962).
8. These are the three key concepts in Louis Wirth's sociological definition of the city.
9. 1960 U. S. Census Bureau statistics as published in the Chicago *Tribune,* March 15, 1961.
10. William H. Lazareth, "Christian Faith and Culture," *Christian Social Responsibility,* ed. Harold C. Letts (Philadelphia: Muhlenberg Press, 1957), III, 40—75.
11. For an interesting analysis by a Roman Catholic priest cf. Andrew M. Greeley, *The Church and the Suburbs* (New York: Sheed & Ward, 1959).

40

12. Cf. Martin E. Marty's use of the term in *The New Shape of American Religion* (New York: Harper and Brothers, 1959).

13. Gabriel Vahanian, *The Death of God: The Culture of Our Post-Christian Era* (New York: George Braziller, 1961).

14. Wystan H. Auden, "For the Time Being," *Collected Poems* (New York: Random House, 1945), p. 410.

15. Thomas S. Eliot, *The Rock* (New York: Harcourt-Brace and Co., 1952), p. 108.

16. For a fine discussion on this point cf. Gabriel Vahanian, "Beyond the Death of God: The Need of Cultural Revolution," *Dialog*, I, No. 4 (Autumn 1962), pp. 18—21.

17. For needed definition and clarification of the idea of secularism cf. Will Herberg's "Religion in a Secularized Society: The New Shape of Religion in America, Lecture I" *Review of Religious Research*, 3, No. 4 (Spring 1962), pp. 145—158.

18. Will Herberg, *Protestant-Catholic-Jew: An Essay in American Religious Sociology* (New York: Doubleday, 1955), p. 15.

19. E. G. Lee, *Mass Man and Religion* (New York: Harper and Brothers, n. d.), p. 33.

20. W. Norman Pittenger, *The Historic Faith and a Changing World* (New York: Oxford University Press, 1950), p. 39.

BOOKS   BIBLIOGRAPHY

Auden, Wystan H. "For the Time Being," *Collected Poems*. New York: Random House, 1945.

Clark, Carl A. *Rural Churches in Transition*. Nashville, Tenn.: Broadman Press, 1959.

Eliot, Thomas S. *The Rock*. New York: Harcourt-Brace and Co., 1952.

Fagley, Richard M. *The Population Explosion and Christian Responsibility*. New York: Oxford University Press, 1960.

Felton, Ralph A. *The Pulpit and the Plow*. New York: Friendship Press, 1960.

Greeley, Andrew M. *The Church and the Suburbs*. New York: Sheed & Ward, 1959.

Herberg, Will. *Protestant-Catholic-Jew: An Essay in American Religious Sociology*. New York: Doubleday & Co., Inc., 1955.

Kloetzli, Walter, ed. *Challenge and Response in the City.* Rock Island, Illinois: Augustana Press, 1962.

Kloetzli, Walter, and Arthur Hillman. *Urban Church Planning.* Philadelphia: Muhlenberg Press, 1958.

Larson, Robert, E. W. Mueller, and Emil Wendt. *Social Changes and Christian Responsibility in Town and Country.* Chicago: Town and Country Church, National Lutheran Council, 1960.

Lee, E. G. *Mass Man and Religion.* New York: Harper and Brothers, n. d.

Lenski, Gerhard. *The Religious Factor.* Garden City: Doubleday & Co., Inc., 1961.

Letts, Harold C., ed. *Christian Social Responsibility.* Volumes I, II, and III. Philadelphia: Muhlenberg Press, 1957.

Marty, Martin E. *The New Shape of American Religion.* New York: Harper and Brothers, 1959.

Niebuhr, Reinhold. *Pious and Secular America.* New York: Scribner's, 1957.

Pittenger, W. Norman. *The Historic Faith and a Changing World.* New York: Oxford University Press, 1950.

Raines, Robert A. *New Life in the Church.* New York: Harper and Brothers, 1961.

Smith, T. Lynn. *The Sociology of Rural Life.* New York: Harper and Brothers, 1953.

Southcott, E. W. *The Parish Comes Alive.* London: A. R. Mowbray and Co. Limited, 1961.

Statistics, Bureau of. *1961 Statistical Yearbook of The Lutheran Church — Missouri Synod.* St. Louis: Concordia Publishing House, 1962.

U. N. Department of Social Affairs, Population Division. *The Future Growth of World Population.* New York: United Nations, 1958.

Vahanian, Gabriel. *The Death of God: The Culture of Our Post-Christian Era.* New York: George Braziller, 1961.

Winter, Gibson. *The Suburban Captivity of the Churches.* Garden City: Doubleday & Co., Inc., 1961.

Whyte, William. *The Organization Man.* New York: Simon and Schuster, 1956.

ARTICLES

Herberg, Will. "Religion in a Secularized Society: The New Shape of Religion in America, Lecture I," *Review of Religious Research,* 3, No. 4 (Spring 1962).

Schuller, David S. "The Impact of American Culture on the Growing Child," *Lutheran Education,* 97, No. 3 (Nov. 1961).

Vahanian, Gabriel. "Beyond the Death of God: The Need of Cultural Revolution," *Dialog,* I, No. 4 (Autumn 1962).

For 125 Years
Toward a More Excellent Ministry

CARL S. MEYER

Concordia Seminary's mission to achieve a more excellent ministry stretches back, over a period of 125 years, to the year 1839. The story began in Perry County, Mo., in a sparsely settled section of the country, not far removed in distance and time from the frontier, among immigrants bewildered in their new homeland and living in poverty. The school transferred its locale to St. Louis after 10 years. There it grew and prospered under the blessings of God. It was concerned for the next century and more with the task of preparing men to become able ministers of the New Testament and to exercise, to the best of their ability, their God-given office. Indeed, the seminary ever strove to train excellent ministers of Christ Jesus, the Head of the church.

Perry County Beginnings

Concordia Seminary's mission or goal was not clearly expressed at its founding. The advertisement which announced its opening to the Germans in St. Louis and the surrounding territory sounded like the announcement of a school that would prepare men for the university. The log-cabin school in Perry County, in the vision of its founders, was to prepare men for all the learned professions. The law, medicine, and teaching were to be served as well as theology and the pastoral office. Their vision, embedded deep in

45

the tradition of Christian humanism, saw learning as a requisite also for the pastoral office. These men were acquainted, after all, with theological departments attached to universities rather than with theological seminaries existing as separate entities. Their hopes for a university in the backwoods of Perry County were not realized because of poverty and because of the demands for ministerial candidates.

There were three founding fathers — Theodore J. Brohm, J. F. Buenger, and Ottomar Fuerbringer. They were candidates of theology who had no parish but valued learning highly. With foresight beyond that which one would look for in young men who had no position of responsibility or leadership in the colony, they set about to establish a seat of learning. The Perry County pastors of their group promised their aid. So it was that Pastor G. H. Loeber, Pastor E. G. W. Keyl, and Pastor C. F. W. Walther gave them encouragement. Only the latter could find a little ready cash to add to the resources of Buenger, Brohm, and Fuerbringer to purchase six acres on which to erect a log cabin. Later in the summer a small sum came from the Saxon congregation in St. Louis, the group of Lutherans who had remained there when the rest of their fellow immigrants moved to Perry County. The heat and the unaccustomed physical labor, the scanty help received from the immigrants who were building their own homesteads, and the lack of financial resources did not deter these young men under the dynamic leadership of J. F. Buenger. The log cabin was not ready for use until early in December. Only 16×21 feet, it was a small beginning for a university.

The school opened on 9 December 1839. There were seven, or perhaps only five, boys who entered the school, and four girls. They ranged in age from five to fifteen. It would be a long time before any of them would be ready for the ministry. It would be a long time, too, before the number would be augmented.

46

One by one the four instructors at the school left Perry County. For a while Brohm carried on the work almost single-handedly. Then he too left by May 1843. A crisis had arisen. Would the school continue? Should it be reorganized?

At this juncture a layman in St. Louis, Mr. Ahner, Sr., encouraged the Lutheran congregation in St. Louis to come to the rescue of the small school. The Rev. C. F. W. Walther by this time was pastor of the St. Louis congregation. He, too, was vitally interested in the continuance of the school in Perry County. After repeated meetings of the congregation in St. Louis and with the cooperation of the congregation in Altenburg, a *de facto* reorganization of the school took place. Johann J. Goenner became the instructor at the school. No longer was the school coeducational; no longer would it aim at providing instruction preparatory for all of the learned professions; it would concentrate on providing a preparatory course and a theological course for those who would enter the parish ministry. Incidentally it might train teachers also.

For the next few years the roster of students remained largely unchanged. Six or seven or possibly eight students can be identified. These young men had their vocational goal clearly in mind. They wanted to serve the Lord in the church as ministers of the Gospel. On 7 October 1847 the first graduate passed his examination and was dismissed from the school. He was J. A. F. Mueller, who as a 14-year-old boy had been among the first students on that December day in 1839 when the school was opened.

Two other men were graduated from that first group — Franz Julius Biltz and Christoph H. Loeber. The former became the President of the Western District of The Lutheran Church — Missouri Synod; the latter, director of Concordia College in Milwaukee, Wis. The third of their number, who, however, had not been with them when the school opened in December 1839, was Heinrich Wunder, a pioneer Lutheran pastor in Chicago, who

47

contributed greatly to the founding and growth of his Synod in the Chicago area and who served as the first President of the Illinois District of the Synod. The fifth graduate of the Perry County school was C. H. R. Lange. He was professor of English and philosophy at Concordia College and Seminary, St. Louis, from 1858 to 1861 and professor at Concordia Seminary from 1878 to 1892. He promoted the study and use of the English language in order that a more excellent ministry might be carried out in the United States of America by these German immigrants.

Only five graduates in a 10-year span! During those 10 years, in 1847, the Missouri Synod was organized. If this church body was to train men for a more excellent ministry, it must have a seminary. It seemed desirable that the Perry County school should be relocated and be brought to St. Louis. On 16 December 1849, 10 years and one week after its opening, the school found a new home in the thriving urban frontier city on the Mississippi.

At Home in St. Louis

It found also a new theological professor: C. F. W. Walther, who had been formally elected to this position.

On 11 June 1850 took place the dedication of the building in which both the faculty and the students lived, in which classes were held, and which served as the headquarters of the Missouri Synod. By 1852 the second wing of the building was built. In 1858 the middle structure was dedicated, and this completed the permanent home of Concordia Seminary, a home that claimed praise from visitors, friends, and well-wishers of the institution.

Between 1849 and 1861 both the preparatory department and the seminary were housed in this building. Under the leadership of Professor C. F. W. Walther, who was formally appointed president of the institution in 1854, men were trained in the languages, in literature and the arts, as well as in theology to serve in the ministry of the church. The preparatory department attracted even a few non-Lutherans who wanted a strong academic training.

In the period between 1849 and 1861 Walther was aided by a number of outstanding men. Chief of them was Professor Adolph Biewend, who died in the flower of his manhood in 1858. He encouraged the study of the languages, also English, and the sciences. Rector Schick encouraged the study of the classical languages.

Between 1849 and 1861 35 men passed their examination for the ministry. During these years, it might be noted, there were six years without any graduates. In one year (1860) 10 men were graduated, the largest class that graduated from the school during this period. It was this class that produced the missionary to California, J. M. Buehler, and the first student, Stephan Keyl, who continued his work at another institution before entering the ministry.

When the 25th anniversary of the Missouri Synod was celebrated in 1872, the 33d year of the existence of the school, only 133 men had been graduated from Concordia Seminary. Of these 133 men 60 were graduated in the five-year period from 1868 to 1872. The quality of the training they received was high; the number of those receiving this training was low. Professor C. F. W. Walther was the main instructor in theology. What help he received came chiefly from Professor A. Craemer, who had come to St. Louis in 1861.

The year 1861, the year that the Civil War broke out, saw the transfer of the preparatory school to Fort Wayne and the transfer of the "practical Seminary," which had been located in Fort Wayne, to St. Louis. This practical seminary remained in St. Louis until 1875. From 1863 to 1875 there were 246 graduates from that department. The large number of graduates was due in the main to the efforts of the Rev. Frederick Brunn of Steeden in Nassau, who devoted himself to the recruiting and training of young men who were sent to North America, there to become ministers in a Lutheran church after further training in the "practical" seminary. For the time, however, they did not receive the thorough training which the men in the "theoretical" department received. Both Walther and Craemer were intent on producing men for a more excellent ministry.

In the 1860s and the 1870s the ideals and the excellence of Concordia Seminary were recognized. In 1857 the young Norwegian Synod made arrangements to train its future pastors in St. Louis. It continued to do so into the 1870s. After the organization of the Synodical Conference of North America (1872) plans were under way to establish one theological seminary for all the synods belonging to that body. It seemed implicit in the plans that the theological leader and the head of Concordia Seminary would be the leader and head of such a joint theological school.

The 1870s were the years in which Concordia Seminary experienced an upsurge. This is true in spite of the defection of two instructors to the Roman Catholic Church. Younger men had been called to instruct the growing number of students. There were Professor G. Schaller and Professor M. Guenther, the biographer of Professor C. F. W. Walther. Professor Lange was called back to St. Louis. In 1878 young Pastor Franz Pieper was added to the staff by the convention of the Synod itself. In that year the Rev. George Stoeckhardt began teaching part time at the seminary. Walther wished, for the sake of the church which he was serving and for the purpose of producing a more excellent ministry, to gather men of scholarship, steeped in Christian humanism, excellent in training, and thorough in their work, dedicated to the tasks which would be allocated to them.

50

Their students must be trained thoroughly in the languages, so that they might read the original languages of Scripture and not be content with the pale light of translations. The church fathers, particularly the fathers of the Lutheran Church of the 16th and 17th centuries, they must read in the original German and Latin. Luther and Baier and Chemnitz and Gerhard were to be firsthand acquaintances. The classroom lectures were in Latin, but German and English were also used. The training was to be theoretical and functional. It was to be steeped in Lutheran orthodoxy and in the study of the Scriptures. The curriculum did not vary during these years, nor was there to be much change in decades ahead. The Scriptures, systematic theology, an acquaintance with the church's past, particularly with the writings of the champions of pure doctrine, the art of preaching and the imparting of catechetical instruction, pastoral counseling adapted to the needs of the people in the New World, these were the studies which would make a more excellent ministry for The Lutheran Church — Missouri Synod.

Further Expansion

An era came to an end with the death of Dr. C. F. W. Walther in 1887. The curriculum of the school was not changed greatly; the task and the character of the school remained the same. The new president and theological leader was Professor Franz Pieper. He was Elisha, who inherited the mantle of Elijah — Walther.

Before Walther died he and Concordia Seminary had weathered the storm of the Predestinarian Controversy. This controversy had scuttled the plans for a seminary which all the synods of the Synodical Conference would support. The two largest synods within the Synodical Conference, the Ohio and Missouri synods, differed on the doctrine of eternal election, and the Ohio Synod withdrew from the Synodical Conference. Now plans were laid and carried out to erect a magnificent new building on Jefferson Avenue in St. Louis to house Concordia Seminary. When the new structure was dedicated on 9 September 1883 almost $140,000 had been spent, a large sum in that day, especially for the erection of a theological seminary. The Synod itself had stipulated that about 10 percent of the cost should be spent on ornamentation for the building, to proclaim the grandeur of the task which was being carried out in this building.

The early 1880s witnessed the establishment of several preparatory schools, which would supply Concordia Seminary with an ever-increasing student body. No longer would the school in Fort Wayne serve as the only one which would feed students into St. Louis. In 1881 preparatory schools were begun in Milwaukee, New York City, and New Orleans. The school begun in New York was moved to Hawthorne (Neperan) and then to Bronxville. The school opened in Milwaukee was to flourish there to the present day. The school at New Orleans was conducted for only a few years. In 1884 another preparatory school was opened in Concordia, Mo. In 1893 a preparatory school was opened in St. Paul, Minn.

These preparatory schools were needed because the large number of immigrants from Germany made it mandatory that the Missouri Synod train an increasing number of men to serve the congregations that were being organized. The Missouri Synod had entered its Middle Period, a period in which it barely kept pace with the population growth of the country. It held fast to many of its old moorings, particularly its language. The same Gospel truth proclaimed by an effective ministry in the first period of its existence was being preached by the men of this period trained also at Concordia Seminary in St. Louis.

During this period new men, of course, had been added to the teaching staff. We can count them on the fingers of our two hands. Ludwig E. Fuerbringer came in 1893 to remain until 1947, a 54-year period. He taught Biblical interpretation and liturgics. His contemporary, A. L. Graebner, had come to Concordia Seminary already in 1887. Although his professorship was of only 17 years' duration (he died in 1904), his impact on the future pastor being trained at Concordia, by his teaching of historical and systematic theology, was tremendous. He had a thorough command of the English language and prepared many men for a more effective ministry during the period of the language transition. Among those who came to Concordia Seminary during this period was also G. Friedrich Bente, professor here from 1893 to 1926. As editor of *Lehre und Wehre,* author and apologist, he had a wide-reaching influence during his time and on the subsequent generation. George Mezger was the last of the men appointed in the 19th century. He came to Concordia Seminary as professor in 1896 and remained here until 1923, when he went to the newly founded seminary in Zehlendorf, near Berlin. His instruction in homiletics trained a generation of preachers whose sermon style was distinctive and effective.

The small number of instructors hardly kept pace with the growing proportion of students. During a 15-year period only one man was called to teach at Concordia Seminary — E. A. W. Krauss. He came from the directorship of Concordia Teachers College in Addison to teach church history, because of the death of Dr. A. L. Graebner. He served from 1905 to 1924. E. Pardieck, who was called in 1912, served only until 1923. Theodore Graebner was called in 1913. For 37 years he was a figure of stature on the seminary staff as editor and teacher in many fields. The year when Krauss was called to the seminary faculty W. H. T. Dau was added. He was a notable student of systematics and history during the years of his tenure, from 1905 to 1926, when he left to assume the presidency of Valparaiso University. Fuerbringer, Pieper,

Graebner, because of their long years of service, provided the bridges from the first generation to the second and from the second generation to the third. The handful of men who taught in the years from 1878, when Pieper assumed his duties, to 1931, when he died, were the men who trained the ministry of The Lutheran Church — Missouri Synod for the difficult years of World War I, the years of cultural assimilation and adaptation to the American scene, the years in which an activistic but orthodox generation took over to lead the Missouri Synod, under the grace of God, to a prominent position among the churches of the United States of America.

During these years the student life, too, was affected by the changes of the world about them. No longer were they required to tend gardens on the seminary grounds, as were the students in the 1850s. Nor were they obliged to go to the Mississippi River to have bathing facilities. The railroad age and the coming of the automobile, the close of the frontier and a trend toward urbanization, the emergence of the United States of America as a world power, affected the externals of the ministry in which these men were to be effective. They went out as circuit riders, *Reiseprediger;* they assumed positions in small towns and villages; they became assistant pastors and pastors of large congregations in urban centers; they opened mission stations in mushrooming suburbs; they went out into foreign countries as missionaries, for their church was beginning to reach out into lands other than the one into which they had been adopted. New Districts were being organized at home, and within the home congregations new groups were being formed. The level of education among the laity was rising perceptibly, especially since the secondary school movement in public education had overtaken and engulfed the academy movement.

The enrollments at Concordia Seminary continued to climb. In 1880 there were 96 students enrolled; in 1890, 136 students. In 10 years the number increased to 193, and by 1910 this number had climbed still further — to 281. Here were the men who were to serve The Lutheran Church — Missouri Synod as pastors and leaders in the first half of the 20th century.

Changes in the 1920s

Among the events of that century few had more far-reaching importance than did World War I. Fifty years earlier the Civil War had profoundly affected Concordia Seminary. Now World War I was to have its effect on this institution. In the decade immediately following this war the "old guard" passed on, and new men took over the leadership of the seminary, teaching a new generation in a language still relatively new to the institution. The 20th century, after 1920 at any rate, would not witness the complacent days which the last decades of the 19th century had seen. After 1920 accelerated changes took place in personnel, in the curriculum, in the complexion of the student body. Only the goal and the means toward reaching that goal remained: a more effective ministry by the sword of the Word — the Law and the Gospel.

In 1922 an "elective fourth year" was added to the seminary. Six men enrolled the first year. They received their S. T. M. degrees in 1923, the first recipients of that degree from Concordia Seminary. During 7 years 63 students were enrolled in this course, which was closed in 1931 because of the small number who had enrolled. It became a victim of the Great Depression. In 1924 the correspondence course was started, a service to pastors in the parish ministry who felt the need of added training. Other changes were reported in 1923: "Lecture courses have been instituted. Students are required to do private reading and are given syllabi for various courses. Working during spare time has been restricted and regulated. The number of English courses has been materially increased." Electives were introduced on a very moderate basis for the men in the second and senior years.

The changes taking place and the advent of a new era were symbolized most dramatically with the building of a new plant. In 1920 the Synod had authorized steps leading to the relocation of the seminary. A new site, the De Mun tract, was purchased on the west edge of St. Louis, in the village of Clayton, in 1921. That same year a building committee was appointed. A new imposing complex of buildings in Gothic style was dedicated on 13 June 1926. Here was a monument of gratitude for the blessings which Almighty God had given to Concordia Seminary since 1839; here was a pledge of faith and trust in future blessings which Almighty God would give Concordia Seminary in the years to come for its task of training men for a more effective ministry.

A new day, a new era, was beginning for the school. Shall this beginning be dated in 1926 with the dedication of the new building complex? Shall it be dated with the death of Dr. Franz Pieper in 1931? Dr. Pieper was succeeded as president by Dr. Ludwig E. Fuerbringer, a symbol of the transition from the second generation to the third. When he assumed the presidency in 1931, he and Theodore Graebner were the only men who had been members of the faculty in 1919. In 1920 John H. C. Fritz was appointed the first dean of students. In this capacity he was also business manager of the seminary until 1940. Fuerbringer, Fritz, Graebner, their colleagues and successors, carried on the work of Walther, Pieper, and their colleagues.

During those years the Great Depression made many modifications seem desirable. The Synod had authorized a "Department of Missions" in 1929, but none was set up because of lack of funds. Nine years later the department of practical theology expanded one of its courses to give more attention to missions and added a two-hour elective in missions. The Students' Mission

Society was encouraged, and periodic lectures were scheduled, to abet the cause of missions. The Lutheran Hour, under the leadership of Dr. Walter A. Maier, its first speaker and a seminary professor, and KFUO, begun in 1924 at Concordia Seminary and housed on its campus, proclaimed the Gospel by modern media of communication.

Summer sessions were inaugurated in 1929. During the 1930s they were held, but only in six of the 10 years. The lack of financial support seemed to hamper the work of the seminary and to destroy its effectiveness. More depressing than the financial stringency was the fact that many of the graduates during these years received no calls. They were laborers standing idle in the marketplace because no man would hire them. There were 114 graduates in 1930. In 1935 there were 153 graduates, but there were only a few calls for these many candidates. What once was regarded as one of the most visible evidences of the blessings of God on the church was now fraught with danger. Who would call these men, and to what places would the church send them? The answers to these questions were not easy, and devices were sought to ease the burden of the great number of graduates. Not until World War II was the number of candidates smaller than the number of calls.

In 1932 Synod passed a resolution that the students at Concordia Seminary should do supply work as vicars after their second year. This arrangement, long optional and now made mandatory, was to prove its effectiveness for the training of men for the ministry and has been retained as a valuable feature of their preparation.

To ease in part the number of men waiting for calls and to give them training to meet the demands of a new age, a preliminary year at Concordia Seminary was authorized in 1935.

In this year the role of the library in the instructional

program received special attention. Not that a library had been neglected during all these years or that its importance had been minimized. Now, however, it was evident that its holdings had not been increased with the increasing output of theological literature. In the 1930s we find an emphasis on the desirability for advanced study on the part of men who would be instructing both in the preparatory schools and in the seminaries of The Lutheran Church — Missouri Synod. Perhaps the "degree consciousness" of American education in general was being reflected in this move. Perhaps it was a realization of the challenges of the day. The granting of a bachelor of arts degree to men who had completed the preliminary year and the first year of the seminary, authorized in 1938, may reflect in part this degree consciousness.

That year, 1938, saw the reopening of the postgraduate department at Concordia Seminary. This department has continued to function to the present day, after its reorganization in 1953 as the School for Graduate Studies. It has emphasized specialized training and research in an endeavor to use all the possible resources of learning for the service of God in His church and for the most effective ministry possible.

Dr. Ludwig Fuerbringer had been an active proponent of advanced study. His successor as president of Concordia Seminary, Dr. Louis J. Sieck, was president of Concordia Seminary from 1943 to 1952; the building which houses the School for Graduate Studies was named after him. Dr. Alfred O. Fuerbringer has been president since 1953, the son of its third and the grandnephew of its first president.

In 1963 there were 46 on the staff, twice as many as had served the seminary during the first 80 years of its existence. The student body in 1963 numbered 590. This was a larger student body than that which was enrolled in 1950, with 526 students, and larger, too, than the 472 enrolled in 1940. Had the school remained stationary in its enrollment? Had it failed to be alert to the new tasks imposed on it by World War II and the atom age? Visions may have been blurred during the years of World War II; the recommendation to close Concordia Theological Seminary at Springfield may be accounted for in this way. Nevertheless, hope and trust continued during those years, and the ideal of training men for a more effective ministry remained. Changes in the program for the improvement and expansion of the church's ability to preach, teach, and apply the Gospel were studied seriously by the faculty, the Board of Control of Concordia Seminary, and the Board for Higher Education of the Synod. The formulation of the objectives of ministerial training, reported to the Synod in 1947 (*Proceedings*, 1947, pp. 155—168), needed implementation by a revised curriculum, a reorganization of the structure of the school system, and added manpower. The high calling of the holy ministry demanded proficiency in doctrinal knowledge, a spiritually dominated personality, a knowledge of man, personal habits, skills, and attitudes, and an appreciation of the minister's functions as an integral part of the Lutheran Church. "It is only natural," it was stated, "to conclude that the longer our Church works in the American scene, the more necessary it becomes for us to approach the natural educational patterns which influence the American public so that our workers will be well equipped to understand the environment in which they do their work and that they will be qualified to lead the majority of the parishioners who are in their charge."

The Present Period

Steps were therefore taken to establish a senior college as a capstone to the preparatory system of the Missouri Synod. The preliminary year at Concordia Seminary was dropped with the opening of Concordia Senior College at Fort Wayne, Ind., in 1957. Simultaneously the curriculum at Concordia Seminary was revised under the leadership of Dean Arthur C. Repp. From 1957 to 1963 the transitional years at Concordia Seminary bridged the third era of the history of Concordia Seminary to the fourth.

The transitional years were not traumatic. The essential task of the school remained. Mingled with new personnel was a core of faithful veterans who had rendered effective service over a longer period of time. The training of chaplains, the clinical training program, the improvement of resident and annual field work, the building of a new library, dedicated 30 September 1962, the strengthening of the School for Graduate Studies and its extension into wider areas of research, could not and did not obstruct the fact that Concordia Seminary was devoted to a program of preparing a more effective ministry for the services of the Lord and His church. God in His grace has given Concordia Seminary 125 years of fruitful service.

Pastoral Training
of The Lutheran Church — Missouri Synod

ARTHUR C. REPP

An effective pastoral training program must rise out of the needs of the church. Since the target of the pastorate has changed considerably during recent decades and since many of the concerns of the present-day ministry have different emphases from those of the past, it is most important that such varying needs and circumstances are reflected in the program which prepares the future clergy for the proclamation of the changeless Gospel of our Lord Jesus. For this task the church must offer the best possible program within its practical limitations. Under given circumstances less than the optimum may effectively serve the church. This must be granted, for there is no single way in which the church must prepare men for the holy ministry.

One of these programs, admittedly not the ideal, is the so-called American plan, with which the majority of American Protestant seminaries have had to be satisfied. For many churches it appears to be the best that can be offered at the moment. According to the "American plan" seminaries must accept college graduates with no particular preministerial training beyond a vague liberal arts program. The general dissatisfaction of seminary administrators and professors with the American plan is well known.[1]

The plan permits the great majority of college graduates to come to Protestant seminaries unequipped for a professional study of theology, lacking not only the basic tools for such a study but often the most elementary knowledge of the Christian religion. For this reason a number of seminaries are proposing that an additional year be added to theological training to meet this general deficiency. These schools recognize that a student coming to a seminary with an insufficient number of college courses in religion is woefully unprepared to study theology professionally. If he lacks training also in the necessary tools to read the theological literature, to say nothing about the Biblical languages with which he is to study the Word of God, his opportunities are obviously circumscribed. Much valuable time is now spent in American seminaries merely to give students the necessary background, especially to equip them with at least one language tool. As a result very little time is left for the serious and professional study of theology.

By way of contrast to the American plan authorities in theological education have had the highest praise for the pastoral training offered at Concordia Seminary, St. Louis, made possible by the preprofessional preparation given at our synodical schools. In comparing Concordia Seminary with the other seminaries associated with the American Association of Theological Schools, Dean Luther A. Weigle, former dean of the Divinity School of Yale, wrote to President Alfred O. Fuerbringer after an extensive visit to the seminary: "You have one of the outstanding theological seminaries of this country and of the world. You have an excellent physical plant and ample room for such further building as your development may require. You have an excellent faculty, large enough in number to maintain a proper faculty-student ratio. Your institution is integrated into the life of your Church, serves the Church, and is supported by the Church to a degree that is notable among theological seminaries." He further stated: "Your requirement of four years beyond the BA with the third year devoted to an internship or vicarage is more adequate than that of many seminaries and is made possible by your close relation to the Church." After a reference to the Niebuhr report which defined the theological school "as the intellectual center of the church's life," he concluded, "I know of no theological seminary which better lives up to that definition in relation to the life of the Church of which it is a part."

What Kind of Person
Is the Minister of the Word?

If theological education grows out of the needs of the church, the question must be asked, What is needed for a minister of the Word as he brings the saving grace of our Lord Jesus Christ to a redeemed world? What understandings, attitudes and convictions, and skills must he have? Perhaps before we answer these questions we must ask, What kind of person must he be? Obviously it is not enough for the minister to have a well-rounded personality, for above all, he himself must be a Christian in the true meaning of that word. Furthermore, he must be a person who chooses to be a minister of the Word out of the conviction of faith which requires him to share the Gospel of Jesus Christ with others and which enkindles in him a continuing desire to prepare fellow Christians for a life and witness of that Gospel. That this necessary motivation may be very weak, or may not even be present, in the 18- or 20-year adolescent must be granted. But it is the continuous task of the schools to supplant whatever wrong motivation may have brought the student to his initial preparation with the more sound and more enduring drive necessary for a mature minister of the Gospel.

In accordance with the wishes of the Synod all schools have adopted a selective admission policy at entrance which is to be followed by a continuous development of the basic personal character, habits, skills, and attitudes which are desirable in the adult Christian and which are essential to the effective performance of the preaching, teaching, and administrative functions of the Lutheran minister. For this reason the synodical high schools and colleges are expected to employ a carefully designed and balanced total program in which the prospective minister of the Word can develop the spiritual, intellectual, social, cultural, and physical capacities needed to round out his total personality.[2]

Pretheological Education

The Unifying Principle of the Curriculum. The only justifiable, unifying principle of the curriculum for ministerial training can be the formal and informal learning in the field of the Christian religion. For this reason it is necessary for the high school and college students to have the opportunity for frequent and intensive use of the means of grace so that by the Holy Spirit's aid they grow in the knowledge of the grace of God in Christ Jesus and in godly living.

Because of the pivotal position of religion, both from a spiritual and from an academic point of view, it is necessary that every student has an adequate preparation in this field before he comes to the seminary. Students who have the opportuntiy to attend a synodical high school or a community Lutheran high school will have had the opportunity for a formal and systematic study of religion beyond the confirmation level. When students begin their ministerial training program on the collegiate level they take an entering placement examination in religion and Biblical knowledge in order to place them in the courses for which they have proper preparation. Students who have a poor factual and conceptual understanding are expected to register for more elementary courses in order to qualify for advanced college work.

66

Rudimentary mastery of religious and Biblical truths is so vital that a student is required to register in preliminary courses when necessary, in preference to going on prematurely in the formal study of the other required courses in religion. Students entering Concordia Seminary will therefore have a high level of understanding of the history and literature of the Bible and several courses in Biblical theology in preparation for their professional study.

Liberal Arts? What Kind? In addition to his preparation in religion the student on entering into his formal professional training must have a broad liberal arts education oriented toward the profession in which he plans to serve his Lord and church. In this liberal arts program much emphasis will be placed on the development of communication skills, so necessary for one who is to be a minister of the Word. For this reason he must not only have the usual opportunities to develop his reading, writing, listening, and speaking skills but understand the principles of general semantics and formal logic as they apply to these skills.

Every student is furthermore expected to exercise the aesthetic appreciation and the humanistic understandings in literature, philosophy, and the arts requisite for a Christian gentleman of culture.

Because a minister of the Word must be a mature Christian who is not satisfied with the "milk of the Word" and must be fed by the strong meat suitable for those of full age and for one who is to be a teacher of others, he himself must become saturated with the Word of reconciliation. For this he must have the ability to use the languages of the Word as it was given to us by God through the holy writers. He should not be left to rely on the interpretation of men as presented through translations. For such a task he needs to be equipped with the basic tool languages, Greek for the New Testament and Hebrew for the

Old Testament. This is essential if the college student is later to acquire the skill to interpret the Scriptures on the basis of the original languages and be able to do this in accordance with sound principles of interpretation.

Why Latin and German? One of the major tasks of the minister is to be able to present the message of the Holy Scriptures clearly for a given situation. As the Christian church throughout its history has been moved to formulate its doctrine through creeds and confessions, so the minister, in an informal but no less important way, must acquire the skill to state the doctrine clearly and precisely. To assist him in this so that he will not lose his moorings from the past it will be necessary that he become steeped in the great creeds of Christendom, particularly the ecumenical creeds and those of the Lutheran church.

He must learn how the great dogmaticians of all ages have expounded the doctrine which they have drawn from Holy Writ. In preparation for this the student must acquire some ability in the church languages, Latin and German, before he comes to the seminary. He must learn Latin to help him later to study the writings of the early church and of the Reformation; German, to help him unlock the treasures of the great Lutheran teachers. While time may not permit him to acquire advanced skill in both of these languages, it will be necessary that at least one of these is reasonably mastered and that a foundation be laid in the other. The knowledge of German and Latin on the part of the Lutheran ministry is an important safeguard for the church of tomorrow so that it may not repeat some of the mistakes of the past. Students of church history can point to the early part of the 19th century, when the Lutheran church in America all but lost its traditional languages and, because of it, fell prey to American sectarianism. No one need think that this may never happen again. In fact, some have already pointed out that this happened to some extent within the past generation when no sound English works of theology, particularly in the practical fields, were available.

The Sciences. Probably more than ever before in the history of the Christian ministry is it necessary for a pastor to possess and use skills and insights dealing with individuals and groups which are based not on simple, native intuitions but rather on an intensive and extensive study of human beings as human beings. Therefore, as a part of his liberal arts education, a student preparing for the seminary must have the necessary skills for dealings with people. In addition he should have the usual courses in the historical development of mankind and some elementary courses dealing with the social, economic, and political problems of the day.

Since the day-to-day developments in man's use and abuse of the natural sciences and resultant personal and social problems raise new and ever more complex problems in the development of an adequate Christian world view, and since the Christian minister has an interpretive function to fulfill for his people, the student's college experience should include opportunities for him to acquire an adequate understanding of the biophysical world and of a mature Christian attitude and judgment toward it. Likewise the important area of physical and health education as a systematic provision for the best physical development and conditioning must be part of the student's continuous experience both at the high school and college level.

Theological Education

With the college graduate's entrance into the seminary his professional training for the holy ministry begins. Here the seminary's task is to provide the church with a ministry theologically and practically competent to minister and to evangelize. For this task the seminary assumes that the student comes with the conviction that he wants to serve his Lord and Savior in the ministry and that he comes with a faith rather than for a faith. In turn the seminary seeks to help him, with the aid of the Holy Spirit through Word and Sacrament, to grow in this faith and in the Christian life, which is a response to that faith.

To provide a competent ministry the seminary must provide a training which is both theological and practical. It has been said that Protestant seminaries teach little more than sermon delivery, teaching methods, and some consulting techniques with little emphasis on content. Whether this observation is correct is immaterial. The fact is that the seminary's obligation is to do both. Its theology must be to set forth the God of our Lord Jesus Christ, who has revealed Himself to man. This theology will not be about "religion in general" but will be a theology that is drawn from the Holy Scriptures as it is set forth in the Lutheran Confessions.

This theological emphasis on "content" will not do away with the "how to" in the curriculum because the Lutheran pastor is a man with a message, a message which must be communicated to people so that they in turn may participate in their ministry of building up the body of Christ. In this dual task the seminary must avoid the extremes of either preparing an activistic ministry or preparing men who have become abstracted from the living church, a condition which has prevailed frequently in the history of the church.

In preparing men for the holy ministry the seminary must be aware that at best it can only introduce the student to a lifelong task. It will make no attempt to prepare the future pastor for a ministry in which he is completely and finally competent. For this reason the theological curriculum has two aspects: (1) a certain number of required courses to lead the student into areas which he needs to explore and to become inter-

70

ested in, and (2) a certain number of electives which allow him a freedom to explore new areas of theology or allow him to go somewhat into depth in other areas.

The required courses help him to experience further some of the broad dimensions of religious thought. This will also assist him in retaining for his future ministry his commitment to a parish responsibility. It is unfortunate that in this age of specialization the parish responsibility ceases to be, for some, a challenging frontier. Service in the inner city, the institutional chaplaincy, social work, campus pastorates, and teaching have come to the forefront in many a seminarian's image of the ministry. Part of the seminary's task is therefore to help the future pastor understand that the parish ministry still remains the greatest single opportunity in the holy ministry.

The curriculum of Concordia Seminary, St. Louis, is divided into the four traditional fields of theological study: the Biblical, doctrinal, historical, and practical. Each of these is dependent on and related to the other, and together they constitute the whole of theology.

Biblical Theology. In the Biblical field, also referred to as exegetical theology, the student studies the total area of Biblical theology. Here he acquires the skills for interpreting the Scriptures. The student learns early as a seminarian that while he will see in his professors expert Bible students in action, his primary concern must be that he himself acquires, on the basis of the Biblical languages, the skill to use sound methods of interpretation so that he will be able to continue to investigate and interpret the Scriptures independently in his parish ministry. The Biblical courses are not intended to give him an official interpretation of certain books or a specific passage of the Bible, but they are to help him, with the aid of the Spirit, to arrive independently at an interpretation that is theologically and Biblically sound.

A course in Biblical interpretation affords him an opportunity in a workshop situation to apply the principles he is learning and to demonstrate his ability to express, in an elementary way, the meaning of the sacred text. He will be introduced to some of the major problems of interpretation and to the various answers suggested by Biblical scholars. The workshop situation gives him skill in the use of the critical apparatus of the Biblical text and such interpretive aids as concordances, Bible versions, lexicons, and grammars. Later through his studies of individual books of the Bible he will get additional opportunities to further the skills initiated in the workshop setting. To acquire a working knowledge of the Bible as a whole, he will study each of the books individually as to content, origin, form, composition, and theological motif. The seminarian further makes an intensive study of several books in both the Old and New Testaments in order to have the opportunity to learn proper method. In addition to courses dealing directly with Biblical themes or books, the student is able in his final year to select, on an elective basis, courses in archaeology, the languages and literature of the ancient world, as well as in readings in the thought world of the New Testament. More than one fourth of the required courses of the ministerial curriculum are in Biblical theology.

Doctrinal Theology. In the field of doctrine every student is expected to acquire an understanding of how the church has formulated the doctrine of Scripture in the light of its varying needs. With this understanding the seminarian is expected to obtain the skill to present the Christian doctrine clearly for his future ministry. During his first year already he studies the entire Christian doctrine in three major courses. These courses are designed to help him acquire a deepened understanding of his church's doctrinal formulations as they are set forth in its confessions and in the Lutheran tradition, including ways in which the doctrine was shaped within its historical and polemical settings. While approaching the study of Christian doctrine professionally, the student himself is strengthened in his Christian conviction. He gains a greater appreciation of the Holy Spirit's work in preserving this theology and in guiding the whole church within God's truth. At the same time the student learns to confront honestly the human conditioning which in any age threatens to blight the Gospel.

During the student's second year at the seminary he studies the Lutheran Confessions intensively in a series of three courses. Here he investigates the historical and theological setting of each of the creeds while analyzing their doctrinal content. During the same year he becomes acquainted with the teachings of other religious bodies of America, particularly some of the modern trends and tendencies. Some attention is given to the vagaries of modern cults so peculiar to the American scene. Because the minister of today will come in contact with some of the major non-Christian religions of the world, even though he may never leave this continent, time is set aside for a fairly comprehensive survey of the major religions of the world. In order to understand the impact that modern philosophy is making on contemporary life and theology, every student is further required to take a course in current philosophical movements.

Historical Theology. In his study of historical theology the seminarian learns to understand the doctrine of the Christian church in its historical setting. Here he sees God's guidance in the ongoing life of the church over the centuries and discovers how the church in every generation has interacted with the social order of its day. Such a study includes more than the history of the church, for it will emphasize particularly the history of its theology, that is, how Christian doctrine was developed during the centuries, how it was variously interpreted, and how it was influenced by its environment. Through his investigation of the

73

church's past the future pastor is helped in his interpretation of the world in which he lives.

During the student's first year three courses are devoted to the history of the church from its beginning to the present. In his second year the seminarian takes two electives, one in the period of the early church and one in the Lutheran Reformation. During his last year he takes an elective in the Lutheran church in America, American Christianity, or modern world Lutheranism. By means of additional electives the student is given an opportunity to concentrate on an important phase of historical theology.

Practical Theology. Because of the many demands made on the parish pastor today great care must be given, as already stated, to maintain the proper emphases in the field of practical theology. There is a danger either of overemphasizing the practical and crowding out the other theological disciplines or of regarding the practical field simply as a series of nontheological "how to do it" courses. This minimizes their importance or, to keep them respectable, tends to make them theoretical so that they fail to meet the day-to-day needs of the parish. Constant attention is therefore given to the proper balance between theory and practice and to the maintenance of a correct relationship of the practical to the remaining disciplines. To assist the teacher and the student in keeping a proper balance, principles and theories of the classroom are combined with on-the-job experiences in the field.

During the first year the seminarian is given his basic training in preaching, worship, and teaching. Each of these studies is closely associated with field work in a local parish under the supervision of a pastor. During his first year the ministerial student engages in two activities a week in a parish to which he has been assigned. The type of work in which the student engages depends somewhat on the courses he is taking at the time.

74

The student's course in preaching is closely integrated with one in persuasive speech. Through individual help in smaller groups the student acquires a skill of communicating the Gospel in an effective manner. Having completed his first course, he is permitted to preach. In the initial course in Lutheran worship emphasis is placed on worship as action, that is, the response of faith. Corporate worship and the approach through the liturgy and the church year are stressed in this course. On the completion of the course the student is permitted to conduct altar services.

Considerable emphasis is placed on teaching during the first year. A practicum is attached to the teaching course wherein all students are required to observe the teaching of religion by a qualified teacher of one of the local parish schools. Toward the end of the course each student is required to teach a unit of religion for five consecutive days. This experience is in addition to the teaching assignment which he may also have in his field work.

During the second year additional courses are given in preaching, worship, and teaching; in addition the student takes a survey course in pastoral theology and a course in the principles of clinical work. All these courses are to prepare him for a year of vicarage. Attached to the course in clinical work is the second year of field work assignment. This includes an opportunity to work in three different areas: hospital, institutional, and inner-city.

During his third year the seminarian serves in a parish for 12 months under close supervision of a pastoral supervisor. During this year he is involved in full-time work in a parish, where he learns to apply the theological training which he has received so far. This year of vicarage, as it is called, is probably one of the most rewarding years of the student's training, since he puts many of the theories he has learned to work. It serves also to prepare him for "the shock" later as a minister; he now

75

experiences the lag between the ideal and the actual church. The vicarage is a year of rapid maturing for most of the students.

During his final year the student's past year of practical experience leads him to choose courses in which he has gained special interest or in which he feels particular needs for his future ministry. All seniors are required to take an advanced course in pastoral theology and church administration and their final course in preaching. During this year the seminarian is expected to take an elective in missions to help him appreciate more fully the opportunities and the challenge of the Gospel as it relates to world issues. Specialized courses in youth work, rural church, urban church, the family, campus ministry, worship, and the like, afford him ample opportunity to round out his seminary training.

What may the church expect from the seminary's curriculum? First and above all, a clergy dedicated to its God and Father through the Lord Jesus Christ, dependent upon the power of the Spirit, and loyal to the traditions of the Lutheran church. Secondly, a qualified ministry that is equipped to function within the varied demands, responsibilities, and opportunities which face the church today. Thirdly, competent pastors who in various ways are able further to equip the Christians who have called them, that they may nurture and build up the body of Christ.

Specialized Ministers

In addition to preparing men for the parish ministry Concordia Seminary has the responsibility of preparing men, and in some cases women, for specialized fields of service. Men and women preparing for foreign service are required to take nine weeks of intensive training before going on to their assignment. This includes training in mission methods, administration, lin-

76

guistics, and an intensive study of the geographical area to which they have been called.

Pastors who desire additional training in clinical pastoral education, either for the parish or for an institutional chaplaincy, may take one or more quarters of training of 12 weeks each in one of the seminary's training centers. Presently there are two such centers, one in St. Louis, Mo., and the other in St. Paul, Minn.

In cooperation with the Wheat Ridge Foundation the seminary offers graduate work in theology for a limited number of students preparing for a doctorate in psychology at the University of Minnesota. Graduates of this program serve the church as counselors in a local congregation while assisting other ministers in their pastoral counseling in the area of mental health.

In a similar manner the seminary assists the Lutheran Social Work Scholarships, Incorporated, by providing lay students who are specializing in social work with additional training in religion to assist them in their future work as Lutheran social workers.

The School for
Graduate Studies

Through its School for Graduate Studies the seminary offers programs of advanced theological studies leading to the master's and doctor's degrees. Here potential leaders of the church receive additional training to serve the church in local conferences and at the District level. The School for Graduate Studies helps provide candidates to serve in the Synod's professional schools, both at home and abroad. College graduates with a major in religion who recognize the need for additional training in theology, particularly those teaching in parish schools and in community high schools, may pursue a program of studies which leads to the master of arts in religion degree.

The School for Graduate Studies offers further opportunities for serious study and research by encouraging the publication of important theological monographs. A division of research is presently in operation which will further help the church by providing theological leadership to those who need to explore new areas of church work in America's fast-changing society.

NOTES

1. See, for example, Paul Ramsay, "Theological Studies in College and Seminary," *Theology Today,* XVII (January 1961), 466—484.
2. The section which follows is based largely on the author's report, as chairman of the Curriculum Commission, to the Synod's Board for Higher Education. The board embodied the report in its own report to the Synod assembled at Cleveland, June 1962 (*Proceedings,* pp. 49—52).

Hear Ye Him:
Training the Pastor in the Holy Scriptures

MARTIN H. FRANZMANN

"Hermeneutics, Isagogics, Exegesis"

"What do you do, Daddy? I never know what to tell people when they ask me," my son once told me. I know that a nine-year-old needs something that sounds impressive, and so I told him, "Tell them your father teaches hermeneutics, isagogics, and exegesis." He memorized that, and the thing served very well to keep the snobs in third grade in their place. But when I am not helping my son to impress third-grade snobs, I much prefer to use something less mysterious and more generally understandable than "hermeneutics, isagogics, and exegesis" to describe my ministry. We have our own technical language, of course, just as carpenters, plumbers, TV-repairmen, and lawyers do, but what we who instruct future pastors in the Holy Scriptures do is at bottom very simple. We teach men to listen.

The Apostolic and Prophetic Word

When our Lord returned to His Father, He left behind Him on earth nothing but the men whom His Father had given Him. He left apostles, witnesses to Himself. Through them He works; in them He continues to speak. We have their Word and witness to the Lord Jesus Christ in the New Testament. If we would hear the voice of the Good Shepherd, we must listen to His

81

apostles; if we would listen to the apostles, we must listen to the New Testament. The apostles witness to Jesus of Nazareth as the fulfillment of the Old Testament Scriptures. All that He was in word and work, they tell us, all that He is, as Son of God, as Servant of God, as the Anointed of God, is fulfillment of the ancient promises of God. The apostles declare that all the prophets of the Old Testament bear witness to Him, that He is God's Yes to all God's promises, that He died for our sins and was buried and was raised from the dead "according to the Scriptures." If we would hear the apostles, we must also hear the Word which they quote, appeal to, and presuppose. We must listen to the Old Testament.

The Art of Listening

We must learn to listen. We who teach exegesis, the interpretation of the Holy Scriptures, must teach men to listen, really listen, to this Word. This is a very simple, down-to-earth sort of thing; we teach men to do what every person does in any conversation. But it is as profoundly difficult as it is simple. We know how hard it is to understand people on their terms, how easy it is to half-listen, to read one's own thoughts into another's words; how readily we misunderstand. And when we consider what this listening to the Bible means, what the difference between hearing and not hearing the voice of our Good Shepherd is; when we consider that this listening is a life-or-death matter for the church, then we realize that the ministry of teaching men to listen is a high and fearful ministry. Then we realize that we must learn to listen (and teach men to listen) consciously, in a disciplined way, in a systematic manner. We must think about and formulate the laws of good listening. These laws of good listening we call hermeneutics. And listening according to these "laws," listening in a highly conscious, disciplined, and systematic way, that we

82

call exegesis. "Isagogics" is a special branch of exegesis, one step in the process of disciplined listening. We shall recur to it later.

Three Barriers to Listening

Listening is an art to be learned even under the most favorable conditions, even when the hearer and the listeners are as close together as they can be: both Americans, say, both English speaking, both on the same educational level, both Christians, both in the same room (even the telephone makes a difference). Here listening and understanding is a relatively simple business. But it grows increasingly difficult as there is less and less common ground (of language, culture, history) between the speaker and the hearer. The first step toward listening rightly is, then, to recognize and face the difficulties. In the case of the voice of the Good Shepherd in the Old and New Testaments there are three barriers to listening. We hear this voice in documents written in Hebrew, Aramaic (a sort of cousin to the Hebrew language), and Greek; there is the barrier of *language*. We hear this voice in books written long ago and far away; there is the barrier of *history*. And there is a third barrier, one peculiar to this Book and this voice, the most formidable barrier of all. We hear the voice of God in this Book, and since Adam's fall we are all like Adam. We want to run and hide at the sound of God's voice. We do not want to face Him in His majesty and mercy. We can call this the barrier of the *flesh*.

The Barrier of Language

Time and history have set up a barrier between us and the voice of the Good Shepherd in the Holy Scriptures. The Gospel has moved westward, and Hebrew and Greek are no longer our speech. But we can hear that voice still; if time has built fences to keep us out, God has built stiles to get us over the fences. The

83

Good Shepherd is as near as He ever was. We have more means at our disposal for mastering the languages of the Bible than any generation in the church before us. Just the last 75 years have seen great advances in the study of the Greek of the New Testament, for instance. We have better grammars than any generation before us; we know how the men of the first century put together phrases, clauses, and sentences. We have better dictionaries; we can know the tones and overtones of the words of Matthew and Paul as never before. (The best Greek dictionary of them all, by the way — and that is the opinion of a Roman Catholic scholar! — was published with funds provided by our own church and was translated and edited by a scholar of our own church, the sainted Dr. William Arndt.) We have excellent concordances, books which list all the words used by the inspired authors, so that we can, in a matter of a few minutes or hours, see how Paul, for example, uses the word "grace" or "justify" or "faith" in all his writings. Thanks to the historian and the archaeologist, we know more about the world in which the apostles and prophets and our Lord lived. When they use pictures from their lives to bring home to us what God is telling us, we can see the picture clearly — the Sower going out to sow, the woman putting leaven into her dough, the athlete training for the contest, the steward administering his master's estate.

These things we can use to teach a man to listen to the one voice that matters and matters forever, the voice of God, the voice of the Good Shepherd, who died for the flock. We can lead a man to look at each part as part of the whole, at the whole as made up of these parts, circling from the part to the whole and the whole to the part until he can see what each part means *in its place* as a part of the whole — and this is most important, to know how and where and in what setting a thing is said. Any married person knows that "Yes, dear" can mean six different things, depending on who says it and to whom and where and

84

when and how. Where and how a thing is said in the Bible can be just as important as the fact that it is said.

"But we have good translations of the Bible. Why not use them?" We thank God for the good translations He has given us. But the question, "Why not stick to translations?" sounds odd to one who has learned a language, odd and meaningless. Ask someone who learned a German lullaby when he was a child why he does not sing it in translation, and you will probably get a blank stare. We cannot all learn the Biblical languages, and it is not necessary that we should. But for those who can — and most people can; they are not at all so difficult as many people think — it would be sheer nonsense not to learn them, nonsense and ingratitude to God.

To be able, with a little effort, to move one step closer to the Good Shepherd, and not take that step? To be able, with a little effort, to hear the voice of the Good Shepherd more distinctly and more fully, and not make the effort? That is nonsense; and for one who is to be a shepherd of the flock of God, to feed the sheep of Christ — for a man with that privilege and that responsibility not to take the trouble to hear the Chief Shepherd in His own tongue — what shall we call it but ingratitude to the God who has given us both the languages and the means of mastering them? The languages are not a burden; they are a gift and a privilege.

The Barrier of History

At its closest the Bible is 2,000 years away from us in history. The ancient Egyptians, Assyrians, Babylonians, Persians, Greeks, and Romans march across its pages. Long-gone figures, like Abraham, Nebuchadnezzar, Herod, Pontius Pilate, John the Baptist, Peter, and Paul, move across its stage. The story which the Bible has to tell, the account of God's mighty acts and God's powerful Word, is tied up with a history long past. In order to hear what the voice of God means for us here and now, we must go back through history and listen to what that voice meant for men then and there.

Again the God of history has given us materials to build stiles across the fence; we can get close to Him still. We can reconstruct the history of a Biblical book in order to see what situation in the people of God called forth a man of God, moved by the Spirit, to speak the Word of God to His people then and there. From notices in Paul's Letter to the Galatians, for example, and from the Book of Acts we can see what threatened the life of the churches of Galatia, what moved the apostle of Jesus Christ to write these furious and terrible words:

> Though we, or an angel from heaven, preach any other gospel unto you than that which we have preached unto you, let him be accursed. . . . If any man preach any other gospel unto you than that ye have received, let him be accursed. (Gal. 1:8,9)

or such words of yearning tenderness as these:

> My little children, of whom I travail in birth again until Christ be formed in you; I desire to be present with you now. . . . (Gal. 4:19, 20)

What moved the apostle to utter such white-hot words of condemnation? What moved him to such gentle and self-sacrificing solicitude? Christ spoke in him (2 Cor. 13:3) in both cases. Unless we take the trouble to cross the barrier of history into the situation then and there, we shall not hear fully or understand clearly the voice of the Good Shepherd speaking to us here and now with a love that cares so much that it must be stern.

We all know the words which Paul quotes from the prophet Habakkuk in his Letter to the Romans: "The just shall live by his faith" (Hab. 2:4). But do we know fully what the

Lord meant by those words when He bade Habakkuk: "Write the vision and make it plain upon tables that he may run that readeth it" (Hab. 2:2)? Translated into present-day terms, it was as if the Lord were telling us: "I shall send the armies of Red China upon America, to punish the sins of America and of the church in America. China shall be punished in her turn, but now she shall serve as the rod of mine anger against America. What you must do, and what all the people of God must do, is submit to My judgment, to wait quietly until My day of judgment is past. That is faith — to lay your life in My hand, unquestioningly and without complaint, to let Me be completely and utterly in charge of your living and dying; by this faith you shall live." By breaking through this barrier of history we can come to listen to the voice of God and learn what Habakkuk meant by faith and what Paul meant. We can know what Habakkuk's song of faith meant and learn to sing it with him:

> Although the fig tree shall not blossom,
> neither shall fruit be in the vines;
> the labor of the olive shall fail,
> and the fields shall yield no meat;
> the flock shall be cut off from the fold,
> and there shall be no herd in the stalls,
> yet I will rejoice in the Lord,
> I will joy in the God of my salvation.
> The Lord God is My Strength,
> and He will make my feet like hinds' feet,
> and He will make me to walk upon mine high places.
> (Hab. 3:17-19)

The Barrier of the Flesh

The third barrier is the most formidable of all, the barrier of the flesh. No man, no son of Adam, *wants* to hear the voice of God; he wants to run away. There are many men who have successfully passed the first and second barrier but have never passed beyond this third one. Skilled in the languages, at home

87

in history, they know the sound and the feel of Holy Scriptures and can reproduce them with uncanny skill. But they have never felt the force of the Holy Scriptures; they have not heard the Good Shepherd speaking in the Scriptures *to them.* They have not been brought low by God's Law, and they have not been raised up by the Gospel of God. They remain, for all their wisdom and eloquence, a sounding brass and a tinkling cymbal.

The way across this barrier cannot, strictly speaking, be taught. We can teach men languages, and we can teach them history; we can give them grades, advance them if they do well, and fail them if they fail to do well. But we cannot "teach" them to deny themselves and follow the Good Shepherd wherever He leads and to remain always within the sound of His voice; we cannot "teach" them repentance and faith — and love. Not that we despair when we reach this barrier; on the contrary, this is when we are most confident. For here God Himself must take over, and He does take over. If we cannot teach here, we can proclaim; we can bear witness. We can put men in mind of their Baptism. We can bring them the witness of their fathers in the faith who followed this voice through shame and suffering, and into death, and never once had cause for regret; who let this voice drown out all other potent voices in the world and listened to it, and it alone, even when it led them into the depths. We can bring to them the witness of their brothers in the faith, our own witness; we can tell them how this Word has spoken to us in good days and bad days, always saying, "Fear not, thou art Mine." We can let our own lives, lives lived under the sound of that voice, witness to them — a high and challenging responsibility. We can take them to the mountain, and there on the mountain God will hide them in a cleft of the rock and will let all His goodness pass before them. God, in and through the Holy Scriptures, will proclaim His name to them: "The Lord, the Lord God, merciful and gracious, long-suffering, and abundant in goodness and truth." (Ex. 34:6)

And so a preacher is born; he comes down from the mountain of God with shining face, eager and able to proclaim the goodness and the severity of God to God's people. He has been with Jesus, and must confess Him before men; he cannot but speak of what he has seen and heard. And so a pastor is born; he has found in the voice of the Good Shepherd the sufficient and healing answer to his every agony, his every cry. He can speak good words, sound words, words of eternal life to the flock over which the Holy Ghost has set him. And he will speak them, for the love of the Good Shepherd lives in him and has become a compelling force in all his thinking and willing.

Unless our preacher and pastor, by the powerful grace of God, passes the barrier of the flesh, his skills in language and his knowledge of history are nothing and worse than nothing; they feed his pride and inflate his ego. But when he has learned to deny himself and follow the voice, then this skill and this knowledge are precious things indeed. By means of them he can go again and again to the then-and-there of God's revealing deeds and words and find in them the answer to the questions and the cure for the agonies of the here-and-now. Then he can hold the cross, that final and complete revelation of the love of God, before the eyes of dying men in these last, dying days of the world. In his preaching the Word spoken long ago and far away to the malefactor on the cross or to the widow's son at Nain becomes a word spoken to us here and now.

The Fortunate Young Man

One gets the impression that many people feel a bit sorry for the young man who is preparing for the holy ministry; even parents and kindly aunts and uncles tend to cluck a bit over the struggling young theologian, to say nothing of those friends of his who are embarking on more "successful" careers. They should save their sympathy for men who need it. The young man does not need it, not if he is really working at his job, not if he is really wrestling with the Angel and waiting for His blessing. His is challenging work; it calls for all the strenuous intuition, all the disciplined imagination of an art, and all the intellectual acumen of a science. It claims a whole man's total powers. His is exciting work; there is much hard routine and brute memory work as there is in anything worth learning, to be sure. But he breathes high mountain air where he works, and his heart burns within him as he listen to the voice whose accents spell the new life of God, the life of the world to come. And his is rewarding work. He has his share of agony, and there are times of dead flatness in his life; but the main current of his life does not run that way. It runs exuberantly, and it sets toward glory. His life moves toward that day when a Lord whose love delights to do men honor will say to him: "Well done, thou good and faithful servant. . . . Enter thou into the joy of thy Lord." (Matt. 25:21)

Christian Doctrine
and the Symbols of the Church

HERBERT J. A. BOUMAN

If you have come this far in the reading of this book, you will have noticed how many-sided the work of the ministry is. The Christian pastor is a precious gift of the exalted Lord Jesus Christ to His body, the church. As Christ's gift the pastor in turn is charged with edifying, or building up, the body of Christ. The pastor has the grand privilege and the holy responsibility of serving people for whom Christ died, so that they may be drawn ever more closely and firmly to their Lord as the Source of all their strength and motivation for a life of loving service to Him and to one another. To accomplish this goal, the Christian pastor must know, and know how to use, the resources with which the Lord has equipped His church. The pastor must bring the Gospel in all its forms: in preaching, in absolution, in Holy Baptism, in Holy Communion, and in words of consolation and encouragement wherever possible. The Christian pastor is expected to be a shepherd, a leader and guide of the flock entrusted to him to train them to be living and healthy members of the church.

That this is no easy task is clear from the many difficulties and distractions of life in the world today, which seem to make living a far more complicated business in our time than it was for our parents and grandparents. The population of this globe is increasing by millions annually, making the available living room ever more crowded. At the same time modern means of transportation and communication have made our world very much smaller. In very dramatic ways the Christian and non-Christian areas are brought very closely together. Non-Christian religions and atheistic philosophies are aggressively seeking converts, and Christianity is often on the defensive. Yet the Christian pastors are in increasing numbers called upon to be missionaries to the world's non-Christian millions.

Even in past generations the education of men for the ministry of the Gospel included many fields of learning and extended over a number of years. With the ever-growing complexity of modern life and the constantly rising level of general education, the scope and extent of pastoral training in our church must try to keep pace so that the Christian pastor may be properly prepared to cope with these conditions.

The Christian pastor is engaged in a ministry to and for people, but, above all, his is a ministry of the Word. The acts and thoughts and words of God to man are recorded in the Holy Scriptures. To know what this Word of God, written by men of God originally in Hebrew, Aramaic, and Greek, is saying to people of our time requires of the Christian pastor that he be a thorough and continuous student of the Bible.

Yes, it takes a lot to be a Christian pastor today. A lot is expected of him. Unending are the demands made on him to do justice to his calling, or better, to provide adequately for the people whom he has been called by the Lord to serve.

To enable him to begin his ministry with some competence and to equip him for continued study, our church, The Lutheran Church — Missouri Synod, has established and is operating its theological seminaries as training schools for the Christian ministry. Thus Concordia Seminary is maintained by our synodical body to function as a Lutheran school of theology. The church expects the young men trained by the seminary as candidates for the holy ministry in the Lutheran church to be prepared to serve intelligently and devotedly as Lutheran pastors. This means that they are the heirs of a specific tradition, schooled in a specific environment, and directed to a specific ministry in the church at large, namely, a ministry committed to the Holy Scriptures and the Lutheran Confessions, or Symbols, educated in a Lutheran seminary for service in and on behalf of the Lutheran church.

Training in Common with Others

This means that the training of the Christian pastor in the Lutheran church will differ significantly from the training imparted to those whose ecclesiastical and confessional environment is of another kind. This does, of course, not mean that the professional training of our prospective pastors is totally different from other training programs. On the contrary, our students are provided with a broad, general education in the common branches of learning, such as languages, literature, the sciences, the arts, history, the record of human thought, in short, all the items that contribute to the general culture in which our men are expected to serve as Christian pastors. Also in the special studies for the ministry in the church our training schools furnish instruction quite similar to that of theological seminaries in other bodies, studies in Biblical languages and literature, in the history of the Christian church, in the skills required for interpreting the Scriptures and preaching their contents, as well as for performing the tasks of the pastoral ministry generally. Yet there is a profoundly important difference in the theological education which the ministerial candidates are offered in our Lutheran seminaries.

Training Different from Others

What is the difference? The fact that our church, with its institutions and schools, bears the distinctive name "Lutheran"

95

suggests that here are certain emphases that distinguish our church from those who bear a different name. This is indeed the case. While all Christian church bodies look upon the Bible in one way or another as source and authority for their religious beliefs and teachings, a number of different ways of looking at the Bible and interpreting its message have come up in the course of the church's history since the days of the apostles. This has resulted in quite a variety of distinct theologies within Christendom, which have become historically established under distinctive labels as denominations. When one hears names like Roman Catholic, Reformed, Methodist, Baptist, etc., one is led to think of so many distinct ways of responding to, and attempting to reproduce the content of, the Bible.

When we thus speak of "Lutheran," as distinct from the other labels, we mean to say that Lutherans have certain distinct convictions about the proper approach to the study of the Scriptures, *proper* not because of preconceived notions of what the Bible *ought* to say, but because the Bible itself suggests it. That is to say, Lutheran theology claims to show *how* one must listen to the address of God in the Bible in order to hear the divine Word to man in accordance with God's own expressed will and purpose. A Lutheran seminary, then, endeavors to impart to its students this considered approach to the Word of God so that they in turn may know *how* to speak the Word of God fully and purely to those whom they have been called to serve. Furthermore, the Lutheran pastor through his distinctive training is equipped to read and understand the story of the church, and of the world into which God has placed His church, from the perspective of God's Word to mankind. And this is where the Lutheran Confessions, or Symbols, come in.

96

The Book of Concord

Martin Luther had an extremely sensitive conscience. He knew himself to be a sinner, and he keenly felt his separation from the holy God because of his sinfulness. "How can I get a gracious God?" became the consuming question of his life. After years of agony and of intensive study of the Bible, Luther was led by the Holy Spirit to discover the forgiving and redeeming grace of God in the incarnation, the suffering, death, and resurrection of Jesus Christ, the Son of God, who took the sins of all men, including Luther's, upon Himself and atoned for them and thereby provided for all sinners, including Luther, a perfect righteousness which is offered in the Gospel and which every sinner receives as a precious gift when he believes God's promise.

As a professor, preacher, and writer Luther taught and preached and wrote his joyful convictions into the hearts of many thousands of people who came to share his understanding of the Word of God. This mighty Christian movement eventually proclaimed its theological convictions and its approach to the Scriptures in a number of official creeds, or confessions, until on June 25, 1580, exactly 50 years after the first official Lutheran confession of faith was presented, the *Concordia,* or *Book of Concord,* was published. This book contains the documents that set forth the Lutheran position in relation to the Scriptures and to other bodies in Christendom. They begin by asserting their agreement with the true Christian faith of all times, as expressed in the Apostles', Nicene, and Athanasian Creeds. Then follow the Augsburg Confession and its Apology, or Defense, written by Luther's friend and chief co-worker, Philip Melanchthon, 1430—31; Luther's Smalcald Articles and Melanchthon's Treatise on the Power and Primacy of the Pope, 1537—38; Luther's Small and Large Catechisms, 1529, and finally, the Formula of Concord, 1577—80.

These, then, are the Lutheran Symbols, the documents to which our Synod, with all our churches and schools, is committed and which give them their distinctive character in relation to other church bodies. When the men trained at our seminaries are presented to the church as candidates for the holy ministry, they are certified as having been prepared for their calling according to the Holy Scriptures and the Lutheran Symbols. And when they are ordained into the office of the ministry, they are asked to assume their charge in commitment to the same position.

The Perspective of the Gospel

What, precisely, is the point of view that distinguishes the Lutheran Symbols from others and gives our churches, our pastors and teachers, a character that identifies them as Lutherans? Following Luther's rediscovery of the true content of God's message to man, namely, the Word of grace in Christ, the Lutheran Symbols affirmed their religious convictions from the perspective of the Gospel. This led them to say that the relationship between God and man revolves around three basic concepts, which were expressed in Latin as *sola gratia, sola fide,* and *sola Scriptura,* that is, "by grace alone, by faith alone, and the Scriptures alone."

These have been called the three *solas* of the Lutheran Reformation. In the church at that time there was much emphasis on the justice of God and His demands that people live up to a certain standard of good works. These works, so the people were led to believe, were then recognized by God as having a certain degree of merit, or deserving a certain reward. Man, so it was taught, was indeed a sinner, but he still had some abilities left to him to cooperate with God in his salvation. If man failed to produce sufficient merit himself, the church could supply what he lacked by drawing on a treasury of merits built up by Christ, the Virgin Mary, and many saints who had done more than necessary. Again, if a sinner did not complete what was required of him in this life, he had to spend a period of time after his death in Purgatory, until the intercessions of the saints and the Masses offered by the church could effect his release. Over against this system of works, merits, and rewards, of offering something to God, as popularly understood, the Lutheran Symbols said, *Sola gratia!* It is God who does everything. The total work of the sinner's salvation is God's. Man had nothing to offer God except his own need and total helplessness. And God acted simply because He is God, merciful and gracious. And God expressed His saving grace in the gift of His Son.

This gift is complete. Nothing can or need be added. No striving, laboring, or offering can make a sinner worthy of this gift. There is nothing to buy or to earn. The sinner must only accept God's gift and trust God's promise. And this the Lutherans expressed by *sola fide.*

Furthermore, since Jesus Christ is our sole and complete Savior and by His redeeming work has made us His own, He is our one and only Lord. There is no other lord and no other authority for His people in the fellowship of the church. None but His voice may speak and demand to be heard. Those who trust in Him are His *free people,* subject only to His gracious rule. No one may usurp His authority and bind men's consciences to demands invented by men. This means that only the Word of the Lord shall be heard in the church, as Luther put it, "The Word of God shall establish articles of faith, and no one else, not even an angel" (Smalcald Articles II, ii, 15). And this is what the Lutheran Symbols intend to express by the phrase *sola Scriptura.*

Therefore a theological seminary committed to the Lutheran Symbols makes the claim that it is training men to be future pastors of the church who desire to give personal and exclusive allegiance to Christ and His Word, in short, the seminary endeavors to shape each future pastor to be "a bishop according to the Gospel." (Apology XXVIII, 12)

The Gospel and Theology

Philip Melanchthon, the author of the Augsburg Confession, the first Lutheran symbol, was also the writer of the first dogmatics, or systematic theology, in the circle of those who shared Luther's views. And this dogmatics, in turn, had grown out of Melanchthon's commentary on St. Paul's Epistle to the Romans, the apostle's most comprehensive treatment of Christian theology. Thus the study and interpretation of the Scriptures, the orderly presentation of Scripture truth, and the confession of faith in the Gospel belong together in the study and ministry of the Christian pastor. The Lutheran Confessions give expression to this relationship of the Gospel to all of theology by means of the frequent use of the formula "We believe, teach, and confess."

A theological education to be well rounded must deal with the Gospel in its total Biblical setting and must provide the answers to a number of significant questions. The Lutheran Symbols, intent upon affirming the Gospel, begin by speaking of God, the triune God, Father, Son, and Holy Spirit, and thus answer the question, "Whose Gospel is it?" and "With whom does it originate?" The Gospel is the Word from the one true God, who is the almighty Creator, who gave all men life and breath and all things, who is the Source of love and every blessing. To do justice to the Gospel means to try to know God as fully as possible as He has revealed Himself, His will, His purposes, His attitudes, His acts in relation to His creatures.

But what is the Gospel? What does it say? To whom does God address His Word? What is man? What is his condition? What are his needs? What is God's will concerning him? What is the meaning of man's existence, and what is his destiny?

100

For what purpose does God address man in the Gospel? What does God accomplish through the Gospel, and what is the nature of its power? How does man respond to God's address? What consequences are there for his life in his relation to God and to his fellowmen?

These are a few of the questions that must be raised, analyzed, and answered in a program of theological study that aims to prepare men to become ministers of the Gospel. This is the task of systematic theology, which purposes to equip the man of God fully so that he may be able to bring the Word of God to bear in all its functions for doctrine, for reproof, for correction, for instruction in righteousness, on all situations confronting the people whom the pastor is to serve.

Necessity of Communication

The Lord of the church has commissioned His servants to preach the Gospel to every creature. The Lord Jesus Christ, who by His death on the cross and by His resurrection has carried out God's plan of reconciling the world to Himself, has given His Word of reconciliation to His church so that the whole world may be exhorted to return to God and be reconciled. The Lord wants all people to confess Him Lord and be His disciples. All people, not only in the days of the apostles but in all the days of this world's history even to the end of the world. This means that the minister of the Gospel must be aware of the progress of the Gospel through the centuries, of the problems of communication, of misunderstandings and perversions of the Gospel, and of ways and means employed by the church in each age to cope with such problems, misunderstandings, and perversions.

In every age the true church has endeavored, under the guidance of the Holy Spirit, to bear faithful witness to the one Gospel of Jesus Christ. To reach the people of its age the church in every age was compelled to explain, define, clarify, restate, and defend the revelation of God and His words and deeds to men. From this activity of the people of God in past ages have resulted the great Christian creeds of the early centuries and later the confessions of the Reformation. In the process of giving positive expression to the truth of the Word of God the church had constantly also to marshal its forces to ward off attacks on the purity of the Gospel. Thus in the course of its history the church strove to give a faithful yes to the Word of God and an equally determined no to all attacks and perversions. With the one timeless Word of God the church had in every time to be thoroughly contemporary so as to communicate the everlasting Gospel effectively. The history of Christian doctrine is of tremendous importance and assistance to the Christian pastor today in his responsibility toward the people of today. His ministerial training must therefore include careful instruction in the ability to formulate God's message in such a way — perhaps in a way totally different from that of former generations — that he may reach the hearts and affect the lives of the people in this age.

Variety and Unity

Many areas of theological study are involved in the training of a Christian pastor, a minister of the Gospel in the Lutheran Church. The curriculum of Concordia Seminary includes a great variety of courses. These are grouped under four general branches of theological education: exegetical, historical, practical, and systematic theology. This listing of departments does not suggest an order of importance. All of them are equally important to a complete ministerial training, and all of them are thoroughly practical. In this chapter the special focus is on systematic theology. Here, too, there are subdivisions, such as symbolics, dogmatics, and a comparative study of all religious bodies.

102

The study of the symbols deals with the "home base," so to speak, of the Lutheran student. In the creeds and confessions contained in the *Book of Concord* the student learns to understand how the early church confessed and proclaimed the apostolic Gospel of Jesus Christ and how the church of the Reformation, sharing Luther's convictions, understands itself in relation to that witness. Furthermore, the study of the Lutheran Symbols gives the prospective Lutheran pastor the direction his ministry is to take in the service of his church. The study of dogmatics is carried on in the light of the church's confessional position. In the same way the theology of other church bodies is examined, evaluated, and compared with the Lutheran stand. Thus as the student prepares for the Christian ministry in the Lutheran Church, he learns to understand the theology both of his own church and of other churches, as well as their relation to each other, their areas of agreement and of divergence, and above all, the presuppositions that shape the various denominational positions. Yet, however much there may be of diversity in theological subjects, there is only a single goal for the training program: to produce men for the ministry of the church, every one "a bishop according to the Gospel."

A Lifetime Task

Much as the seminary strives to provide a comprehensive, well-rounded training for the future Christian pastor, it must not be imagined that the years of study at the seminary have brought the program of theological study to a close. If the seminary has succeeded in equipping the candidate for the ministry with the competence for serious theological study, with the confessional conviction and orientation for his ministry, and with a sense of unreserved commitment to the Lord Jesus Christ and His church, coupled with an unquenchable thirst for continuing systematic study throughout his ministry, the seminary may feel that it has achieved its objectives.

In all the days and years of his ministry in and for the church the Christian pastor will dedicate himself to performing all his work according to the Gospel, in his study and in the pulpit, in all his dealings with individuals and groups in the parish and the community, in public and in private, by word and deed. Only one purpose will animate the Christian pastor: to train a people according to the Gospel. Amid the ever-changing conditions in the world and in the church, the ever-shifting winds of theological opinion, the ever new attacks by means of which Satan will attempt to ensnare the people of God, and the ever new opportunities God will provide for the proclamation of the Gospel, the Christian pastor will feel the need and the desire for never-ending study of the Holy Scriptures and the Lutheran Symbols. Besides, he will ever strive to keep abreast of current developments, so that he may be at all times and in every way "a bishop according to the Gospel," to the eternal welfare of his people and to the glory of the great God and our Savior Jesus Christ.

Missionary Training at Concordia Seminary

WILLIAM J. DANKER

In recent years Concordia Seminary has demonstrated its alertness to the growing Protestant conviction that mission is not a peripheral concern of certain hobbyists but central in the life of the church. There is a growing awareness that, while not every basic function in the church has a direct missionary intention, each of them has, as Lesslie Newbigin has well said, a missionary dimension. Every function has an educational dimension, as well. Teachings and missions belong together ever since our Lord said, "Go ye and teach all nations."

The Lutheran Church — Missouri Synod has from its inception emphasized the church's function of witness. The incorporation of missions in the curriculum at Concordia Seminary is rooted in theological as well as practical premises. Although there have been low points when witness was thought to consist primarily in avoiding contact with other Christians, at its best this meant sharing the Gospel in all its truth and fullness with others. Such sharing involves listening as well as speaking. This was the spirit in which C. F. W. Walther founded *Der Lutheraner.*

The missionary dimension of witness has need and opportunity to come through in many parts of a seminary curriculum, e. g., in systematics, which is to be a device for sharing the Gospel with others in organized form. Always it must guard against becoming a way of imprisoning the Good News. Exegesis is the science of mining the message for the mission rather than a game of analytical and documentary one-up-manship. Historical theology traces the expansion of Christianity from Palestine to the ends of the earth. In all candor church history must relate what, for the most part, has been the tale of a disobedient church and an unfinished task. All the skills of practical theology have a missionary dimension even when they seem to be directed inward toward the edification of the Christian community.

From the days of Daniel the worship of the church has had a missionary dimension. The ministry to the total man in his total setting has never been such a significant dimension of the mission as today. This awareness is found also in the heightened emphasis on medical missions in recent years. Fellowship between Christians has been propelled front and center on the stage of the Christian world mission through the ecumenical movement, which, in many ways, is one of the most noticeable reflexes of the outreach into all the world. And always theological students are reminded that they go forth to be not lords but servants in church and world.

Changing times require no change in the basic functions of the church in its world mission. Changing times do, however, require changing forms. The fundamental architectural dictum that form follows function had its application to the work of the first great missionary who crossed the frontier from Judaism into the Gentile world and to the labors of every missionary pastor since then as he moves across cultural, geographical, and social boundaries, to say nothing of the most important border of all, the constantly moving frontier of time in the most rapidly changing age the world has ever known.

Historical Development

The historical development that led, ultimately, to the establishment of a chair of missions at Concordia Seminary was a process of slow maturation. Missions had been so prominent in the thinking of the men who organized the Missouri Synod that the first board they set up was a mission board. It had the specific responsibility of mission to the heathen, in the first instance the Chippewa Indians of Michigan, as well as the charge to gather the scattered German immigrants. We are only now returning to their breadth and wholeness with the establishment of one Division of World Missions in the structure of the Synod and tentative resolutions on the creation of a single Board of World Missions.

Down through the years Missouri's vision of her mission to the heathen grew dim. The very success of her urgent mission to gather immigrant believers *(Sammelmission* among the German *Glaubensbrueder)* heightened her preoccupation with herself at the expense of her mission to other peoples overseas. When after prolonged prodding the Synod at last embarked on overseas missions in India in 1894, it suddenly found that its theological students had little or no interest in going overseas. This was, of course, natural, since they were the products of a church that had become nonmissionary after an auspicious beginning. For the first two decades it was forced to rely largely on men recruited in Germany rather than St. Louis or Springfield. Beginning at the turn of the century one finds periodic synodical resolutions encouraging the giving of lectures on missions at the St. Louis seminary. The inclusion of missions in the seminary program from these extracurricular beginnings to the establishment of, first, an instructorship in missions and then a chair of missions at the Houston convention in 1953 always had the immediate purpose of boosting lagging recruitment for overseas fields. There was apparently little consciousness until the past decade that the Christian world mission is a profound concern and activity of every parish pastor and every Christian wherever he serves, that the frontier between faith and unbelief exists everywhere and that the home base of the mission is everywhere — in Tokyo as well as in Toledo, in Madras as well as in Minneapolis, in Calcutta as well as in Chicago.

Not an Elective

Missions is not an elective at Concordia Seminary in St. Louis, because to make it such could give students the false impression that missions is an elective in the life of the church. Every student chooses one of several courses in the area of the Christian world mission, such as *The Christian Mission in the World Today* or *The Gospel and World Issues.* In addition, in this age of global mobility, rising nationalism, and resurgent non-Christian religions, it is important that Christian pastors, who are supposed to be experts in religion, know at least the rudiments of the non-Christian religions. Every student takes a 3-hour course in *The History of Religions,* emphasizing Hinduism, Buddhism, and Islam.

Cocurricular enrichment includes the activities of the World Mission Council, which arranges for the highlighting of world missions in special programs and lectures, dormitory and chapel devotions. It presents to faculty and students a wide range of representatives of the Christian world mission. Retreats on mission and days of prayer for missions have frequently been held. In cooperation with the World Mission Council, a voluntary group gathers gifts for specific mission projects from the students and solicits their prayers. It was known as "110" in the past, because shortly after the war 110 students banded together to support a vicar in Latin America. This program continued for about 15 years, during which vicars were supported chiefly in Latin America but also in the Far East. In 1962 the program was rebaptized *Panta Ta Ethne* (All Nations), perhaps because the first of a new series of projects raised some $3,000 to encourage the Western District to call a full-time pastor for All Nations Church, an inner-city mission in the heart of a great St. Louis high-rise apartment development.

Possibly the most effective missionary training, also for eventual overseas assignment, is that which the field work department at Concordia Seminary, under the aegis of Dr. Kenneth Breimeier, administers. Large numbers of field workers have been assigned also to inner-city churches, where the need and opportunity for workers is greatest and where students face the constant challenge of speaking the mighty acts of God to people of other cultures. Here especially they deal with the basic human and divine realities. Field workers who have ridden what *Time* magazine terms the uriniferous skip-stop elevators of the high-rise apartments and spoken the Gospel in homes where there is no lack of children but a great scarcity of husbands may be expected to adjust to a wide range of conceivable future demands. The vicarage program is also an essential part of training for service in the Christian world mission. The best missionary education happens when people see missions in action with their own eyes, or better yet, when they themselves engage in it purposefully and with ongoing supervision and direction.

Missionary Training

In addition, the professor of missions serves as director of missionary training, and this makes him responsible for a school for outward-bound missionary candidates each summer. During a 5-week period each student takes two basic courses. In *Missionary Life and Work* we enrolled 53 students in 1962. Here we face a teaching challenge of the first magnitude. Educational background ranges from high school to S. T. D. Vocations range from builders to nurses, medical doctors, teachers, seminary graduates, as well as the wives of all of these. The common denominator is the missionary life and work into which they go. They are generally remarkably teachable because there is a high index of felt need. More important than the imparting of information is the shaping of attitude and the development of the mission school as an "intentional community" amid the larger fellowship of the summer school. The group feeling is helped by cocurricular activities of various types, climaxed by a final Communion service just before they leave to go their separate ways to the ends of the earth. In the past several years inner-city field work has helped prepare middle-class missionary candidates survive "culture shock" overseas by introducing them to the different standards of another society.

In 1962 and 1963, as one direct result of my study tour of Asian mission fields the previous winter, we conducted a 2-week linguistics institute for all missionary candidates, and this is likely to become an annual fixture because it was so well received. Here students do not learn the language as such, but they do find out how to take a language apart, as it were, with a screwdriver and a monkey wrench, and learn more rapidly and with deeper understanding.

Some mission candidates are given extended specialized preparation before going abroad. Most missionaries to the Muslims attend the Kennedy School of Missions in Hartford, Conn., for thorough orientation. We are studying the possible use we could make of other existing facilities for many of our mission candidates.

As director of missionary training the professor of missions, in consultation with mission executives and boards, seeks to direct mission candidates to such institutions and learning experiences as would best fit them for the tasks to which they have been assigned.

The Role of the Missionary

More and more the missionary is the fraternal worker, the trainer and developer of national workers, the playing coach on an international team, and sometimes just a team member working under national direction. Does this mean that quality is less important than formerly? On the contrary, it means that quality standards are higher than ever before. As John R. Mott of the Student Volunteer Movement used to say, "Greater is he that multiplieth the workers than he that doeth the work." The bright young men of Asia and Africa are hotly eager for education — and sharply critical of those who cannot provide it. At a conference with Japanese pastors and theological students one candid candidate asked, "Why do you send us some missionaries who are so shallow in theology? They are good cooperators, and administrators, but they don't know much theology." A few of our finest graduates from St. Louis assured me that the young Japanese pastors were ardent students, fully their equals in Greek and Hebrew. Some Japanese pastors, on the other hand, tend to lag in the practical pastoral attitudes and skills, in European style.

It is understandable, therefore, that mission boards have set their missionary standards very high in their policy statements.

Recruitment of Missionaries

If providing the worker is part of preparing him, recruitment is within our purview. More selective recruiting is needed. Plenty of first-class all-American boys and girls are needed. However, the mission boards could use a great many more Canadians than they are getting. Commonwealth citizens are welcome in many places where Americans are not. It has been hard to shoehorn American evangelistic missionaries into India. When Castro expelled a group of Canadian priests from Cuba, he had to invite them back and pay their return fare besides. [Canada was still trading with Cuba.] Meanwhile, all our American Missouri Synod pastors have been forced to evacuate. The only ordained pastor is a colloquy candidate of recent vintage who, fortunately, has European citizenship. When he was called to another congregation recently, the president of the congregation had to install him. There was no one else to do it. In other congregations men without formal seminary training are preaching.

In 125 years Concordia Seminary, St. Louis, has graduated only two Negroes. One of these is in the ministry at this writing, the other teaches in a Lutheran university. The church could use a good many able Negro pastors today in this country and abroad. The presence of Negro missionaries on our staffs overseas could conceivably make it easier for our hard-pressed missionaries to answer the embarrassing questions raised by Birmingham, Oxford, and Little Rock, names that are painful headlines especially where men are not white. We need not let the U.S. State Department have all the superior Negro students. It is encouraging to note that there are numbers of Negroes in our preparatory schools and at our sister seminary at Springfield, Ill.

The Image of the Missionary

We invite those who shape the training of our future workers to help us reshape the image of the missionary in the minds of students. He is regarded by turns as a saint and an incompetent. Reinhold Niebuhr in his noted chapter on "The Relevance of an Impossible Ethical Ideal" lifts out the missionary as the Protestant equivalent of the Roman Catholic saint.* When an able graduate student received a mission call his lovable little mother journeyed all the way to St. Louis to ask in touching candor, "Now please

---

* Reinhold Niebuhr, "The Relevance of an Impossible Ethical Ideal," *An Interpretation of Ethics.* (New York: Harper, 1935).

114

tell me the truth. Did you assign him this call because he isn't good enough for a call in this country?"

Stephen Neill, noted missionary scholar and ecumenical leader, says in *The Unfinished Task* that when he with his Cambridge background volunteered for missionary service in India one highly placed churchman after another counseled him not to throw his life away. After he got to India and talked with other gifted missionaries he found that they had had the same experience. No doubt, these churchmen would have given St. Paul the same advice.

We seek to reshape the image of the witnessing, missionary task for all our workers. In earlier, slower times our generals could go right on preparing for the last war instead of the next one and still, somehow, manage to win. Change is nothing new. What is new today is the rapid acceleration of change.

Everybody Is in the Act

Everybody is in the world mission act today. There is no question about their need and their opportunity to witness to people from the ends of the earth. A schoolmate from Buffalo wrote for Japanese catechisms to supplement his adult instruction of wayfarers from the East.

There are more than 60,000 international students in the United States plus countless tourists, business and professional people. If we really tried, more Muslims could be won in the U. S. A. than in the entire area from which they come. Here for a time they are free from the theological and sociological totalitarianism of the Islamic church-state.

Our people are moving overseas in increasing numbers. We have only about 400 missionaries and wives overseas. Perhaps 20,000 of our members are there with the military and in other capacities. We shall not win the battle with the hundreds if we neglect to utilize the thousands. Every pastor's and teacher's job includes training people for their personal global witness. We need a generation of great missionary pastors in the mold of Wilhelm Loehe, who made his little village church at Neuendettelsau a blessing to the ends of the earth. Every pastor and teacher is running a training school for world missionaries. I did not always realize this in the 11 years of my stateside ministry before I went to the Far East. It was unforgettably driven home to me when three boys from the same confirmation class at my last parish stood at my door in Tokyo. One was in Air Force blues, the second in a Navy uniform, and the third in Army khaki. Each of us had gotten to Tokyo by a different route. Just a few years earlier we had drilled the catechism together in West Chicago's Trinity Church basement. After they had left, I began to ask myself how well I had really prepared them in confirmation class for their personal world mission.

Leaders associated with the new Division of World Mission and Evangelism in the World Council of Churches, in their provocative recent study *A Tent-Making Ministry,* raise a whole series of problems for a church that has long followed the classic European pattern of ministerial training. Should we gear ourselves to give the finest possible theological training also to technologists and businessmen who will be passing through doors, e. g., in the Muslim world, that are tightly barred to the professional missionary? The need of developing new forms to carry out the fundamental missionary function will force us, moreover, to study carefully the role of Concordia Seminary in training the great lay apostolate.

The Challenge

All along the route from recruitment through every level of training it is important to challenge men and women to serve God sacrificially and where the task is often hardest — at

116

the growing edges of the church. It is a law of physics that it takes more energy to start a wheel spinning than to keep it going. The most gifted workers should be challenged to tackle the biggest jobs, not necessarily the biggest stateside churches or the biggest stateside schools. Winning people from death to life is a super-human task anywhere in the world; but the reshuffling of church memberships is not as difficult as hacking a soul out of the solid granite of Islam or extricating one from the weblike Buddhist society of Japan. One lad at St. Paul's College, Concordia, Mo., kept pestering his professor with the ancient chestnut, "What about the heathen who never heard the Gospel?" Whether out of exasperation or genuine mission concern we cannot be sure, but the professor finally shot back: "If you're so concerned about the salvation of the heathen, why don't you do something about it?" That young man became a missionary to Nigeria.

At every level we seek to fight professionalism. Kierkegaard said, "The early Christians died for Christ. We live on Him and some of us rather well." James Michener repeats what is often said of the early missionaries to Hawaii, "They came to do good, and they did right well." *Time* magazine recently was at pains to point out that many ministers of the Gospel are doing right well. Every seminary president knows how difficult it is to recruit qualified faculty members, in part because some congregations are ministering so well to the minister. Shall the churches give up their role of challenging people to sacrificial service and yield it to the government with its overseas and domestic peace corps, modeled on the lines of foreign mission service?

Missionary motivation sometimes drains away en route. Dr. Wolfgang Bulle, executive secretary of medical missions of The Lutheran Church — Missouri Synod, says that 40 percent of those entering medical school at Washington University in St. Louis want to become medical missionaries. By the time they graduate, most of them want to make $30,000 a year.

What is the place of missions in the curriculum? Arno Lehmann, who has the chair of missions at the University of Wittenberg-Halle, likes to say, "The professor of missions is the most expendable of all faculty members." Every church is a mission. Every Christian is a missionary. Every instructor is a professor of missions. Those who examine syllabi can look for the missionary dimension. For example, Kenneth Scott Latourette has shown how effective it is to present church history not so much in intramural terms but in the framework of the expansion of Christianity.

An important symbol of the penetration of missions into the total life of the school was the integration of the former mission library into the growing collection of the fine Fuerbringer Library.

"Where in the World
Am I Going?"

Preparing workers for overseas missions includes placement. In the new version of *Mutiny on the Bounty* a ship's officer introduces Captain Bligh to the crew, "A prime lot. No volunteers."

There will always be room for volunteers in the overseas mission. Already Dean John H. C. Fritz's *Pastoral Theology* declared that pastors should feel perfectly free to volunteer for missionary duty. Nearly all other Protestant and even Lutheran bodies must content themselves with volunteers. It is the strength of Missouri that our system of calls and assignments permits us, in addition, to do something akin to what government does in its particular kind of warfare, namely, to draft the best for the supreme test.

Our sister seminary at Springfield has been doing that particularly in the last several years, and we trust that St. Louis will keep up with them. In their excellent report on a recent study trip to Africa Professors Arvin Hahn and Kenneth Schueler emphasized the importance of securing men of the very highest quality for service overseas.

We attempt to condition students from the start to expect placement anywhere in the world. They should be taught to wonder, quite literally, "Where in the world am I going?" The student at West Point knows that he is vulnerable to assignment anywhere in the world upon the graduation. Why should a student at one of our schools be permitted to labor under any different assumption? We must cultivate the outward-bound mind set.

Nor will they actually be going very far away. New Guinea is nearer now than California was in Walther's day. America's incomparable jets fly the Pacific nonstop from Tokyo to San Francisco in 9½ hours. In many instances parents are visiting their missionary children on the field.

We must also beware of the development of another assumption that on call day "East is East, and West is West, and never the twain shall meet." Also the graduate assigned to a stateside position should live in expectancy of a possible overseas assignment. Frequently a few years in the States will give valuable experience and added maturity. An overseas call can come at any time in a pastor's career. While he is at the seminary we try to condition him for that possibility.

To match the population explosion in our world we need a missionary explosion in Christendom and in our own Synod. The training institutions of our church will, we are confident, play an increasingly vital role in the coming missionary explosion. This is also the image which our constituency expects our schools to project on the basis of honest performance, namely, one of all-out involvement in the task of training their students for their particular role in the total Christian world mission.

119

The Pastor as a Person

LEONHARD C. WUERFFEL

> Lord God, Thou hast placed me in Thy church as a bishop and pastor. Thou seest how unfit I am to administer this great and difficult office. Had I hitherto been without help from Thee, I would have ruined everything long ago. Therefore I call on Thee. I gladly offer my mouth and heart to Thy service. I would teach the people and I myself would continue to learn. To this end I shall meditate diligently on Thy Word. Use me, dear Lord, as Thy instrument. Only do not forsake me; for if I were to continue alone, I would quickly ruin everything. Amen.[1]

Every faithful pastor who has served his Lord as a minister of the Gospel for any length of time will agree that this prayer of Luther takes on added significance with the passing of the years. The older he grows the more he knows how dependent he is upon his Lord Jesus and the grace and strength which his Master alone can give. When the apostle Paul confesses: "I am less than the least of all saints" (Eph. 3:8) and when he states: "We have this treasure in earthen vessels that the excellency of the power may be of God and not of us" (2 Cor. 4:7), the pastor who knows himself for what he truly is in the sight of God hastens to agree and uses Luther's prayer with ever-deepening appreciation and meaning. Well does he know how much depends on his personal faith and growth in Christ as he faithfully attempts to lead men to the Lord and keep them strong in the Christ of their salvation. Not only does he of all people know what a weak instrument he is in the hand of God, but he is also supremely conscious of the need for continual learning. With his people he too presses toward the mark, for the prize of his high calling in Christ (Phil. 3:14). Every pastor sensitive to the potentials involved in his earnest endeavors to serve his Lord in serving the Lord's people will only too readily recognize his personal unworthiness for this opportunity and will yearn for the growing awareness of the Spirit's power and presence in all that he does by Word and Sacrament. Particularly will he pray that as a person he may dwell among his people as a worthy example of Christ, in faith and as a man of God.

Parents in the Life of the Pastor

Even before his formal schooling begins the average pastor has received much of the training for his future work as a minister of Jesus Christ. The influence and upbringing in his home is a most essential element in his preparation for his lifework. At a time when many homes are being blasted by divorce and other divisive influences, it is a blessing of God that the vast majority of the future pastors still come from homes where they were taught early in life to love their Lord Jesus and to worship Him in Spirit and in truth.

The strong and steady influence of a God-fearing mother has had telling effects in the development of many a young man as he aspired to become the Lord's man. Much could be said about the prayers of faithful mothers. The story of Hannah has many counterparts in daily life. Equally striking are the imprints made upon many a young man by the dedication and labors of a believing and self-sacrificing father, who also prays that his son may grow up to be a faithful and diligent shepherd among the Lord's people.

Though the number of ministerial students coming from non-Christian homes appears to be on the increase, there can be no doubt about the wholesome and positive influence of a Christian training from early childhood into youth. This is truly a genuine asset for the ministry and a goal to be kept in mind by all Christian parents. Rightly understood, the ranks of the ministry have always been kept filled when fathers and mothers prayerfully and gladly dedicated their sons to the work of the ministry, asking God's blessings and the holy influence of the Spirit upon their aspirations and hopes as well as demonstrating their sincerity by the sacrifices needed to finance their sons' education to that end.

Here is where the image of the ministry is most frequently developed by the very attitude of parents toward their pastors and their readiness to thank God for the blessings of the ministry of the Word as they make use of it in daily living. A story could be written about those faithful parents who not only willingly gave their sons to this cause but also quietly and with no fanfare sacrificed personal comforts to see the objective achieved. The principle of the Lord's observation in the story of the widow's mite could be repeated again and again today if the Lord would deign to have the record revealed in writing in the 20th century. Only eternity will fully disclose the degree of dedication and sacrifice involved in helping sons prepare for service to the Lord as ministers of the Word.

Influence of Own Pastor

In all studies of the ministry it still remains a fact that a young man is most frequently influenced to consider the ministry as a vocation by the life and work of his own pastor. From early infancy the image of the ministry makes its impression, and usually in terms of the person of the man. If father was a pastor the son would quite naturally be given a strong impulse also to become a minister. Studies indicate that as far as influence toward the entrance into the ministry is concerned the pastor is rated highest.[2] "In this decision he was primarily encouraged, as self-reported, by his pastor and mother and father, in that order."[3] In a doctoral dissertation, recently (1961) completed, the author also found that most seminary students gain their understanding of the minister's work from the minister in their home congregation and from the ministry which he reflected into their lives.[4] Pastors' sons are especially prone to think of the ministry only in terms of their father's own pattern of activity and service. All of which points up two things: the influence of the pastor as a person in leading young men to think of becoming ministers and the importance of the total field work program for the seminary student. This aims, among other things, to broaden his experience and by personal involvement to aid him in gaining a better and fuller grasp of what the work of the ministry really is.

When all is said and done it remains true that the pastors themselves are the one strongest influence in prompting young men to consider dedicating themselves to the work of the ministry. It hardly need be stressed that the pastor as a person serving among his people is the greatest contribution to the image of the minister and his work. This image will either add to or detract from the way in which people will regard the importance and influence of this service. Also in this respect the words of Gustav Jensen are apropos.

> From a spiritual man thousands of impulses go forth to other people. The holy process which is going on in him propagates itself with remarkable vigor, even without his particularly being aware of it, through an accidental encounter, or a word which has been uttered without particular deliberation in the midst of the business of daily life. For what he is, he is

always. In this way it has come to pass, as we have observed quite often, that some ministers who are less gifted than others still have accomplished great things in the congregation and have kindled a fire there which cannot be extinguished.[5]

Other Influences Toward
Entering the Ministry

In a recent study of one of the classes entering the seminary it was clearly indicated that in addition to parents and home pastors others also encouraged the students in their decision to enter the ministry. The strongest influence in this study proved to be the student's own mother. Second in strength was the pastor of the home congregation, and third in strength proved to be the student's father. In not a few instances other ministers and teachers had a strong influence upon the student's decision to become a pastor. Some of these pastors were met at Walther League camps or similar occasions of contact. Among the teachers some were Sunday school instructors, day school teachers, or even high school staff members. In a fairly substantial degree brothers and sisters exerted a salutary influence on some of the students and were rated as exercising a strong encouragement in the making of the decision. In a less marked degree others were also listed, friends and older seminarians, aunts, uncles, grandparents, laymen, employers, and wives. The records of the seminary will reveal that in a few isolated cases a dedicated layman has encouraged and supported a student's decision and his ultimate entrance into the ministry. We make bold to suggest that this type of lay activity can be increased in the future for the benefit of the church and its ministry. It may become necessary to a much greater degree for a more concerted effort to be put forth on the part of pastors and their lay people to seek out promising young men and to encourage them to become pastors. To overcome the ever-increasing costs involved additional steps may need to be taken to support such young men as they show their interest in serving the Lord in this way.

What Happens at the Seminary?

In addition to a sound theological training in their formal classroom work the students need help to develop wholesome personalities and in every respect to become the type of person who can serve effectively among the Lord's people. Tom Allan in his publication strikes at the heart of the matter when he writes:

> Ministerial leadership in its deepest sense is in fact only possible when the minister is most truly one with his people, their servant for Christ's sake, and realizing that the work of God in his parish is not his own exclusive responsibility but the corporate task of the community of which he is the representative.[6]

Further careful study will undoubtedly reveal that one of the truly strong contributing factors to the unity among the pastors of The Lutheran Church — Missouri Synod as well as one of the elements that account for their development as persons is the long-standing tradition of a resident program at all the schools preparing pastors for the church.

For many years most men started their preparation in one of Synod's schools at the freshman high school level. In recent years a considerable percentage of the students entered after high school and a much smaller number after some years of college training. We hasten to add that the fact remains that simply to have a set of buildings that will house, feed, and provide library facilities and the other needed physical structures will not guarantee an effective environment for growth. All these blessings need to be focused upon the fact that a body of people dwell here and that they use to the maximum the opportunity of living together as men in Christ. From the president on down to the humblest clerk on any staff of helpers or students all must be agreed as to the purpose of their existence and must translate into daily living the blessings enjoyed as a people of God and as those dedicated to achieving a better ministry for tomorrow. Standards guiding us each day need to be evaluated carefully and usually for the sake of progress need to be raised with each new challenging change in the world at large. In short, as the demands made upon ministerial services and leadership are increased, so the standards governing the training of the men for the task need to be restudied and revamped to meet existing conditions.

One of the unquestioned blessings of a resident program is the total group process in giving direction to all phases of the school's purposes. The quality of the school and its effectual influence will depend on the degree to which all elements that compose it have learned to grow together in Christ and with the guidance of His Spirit have dedicated themselves to the sole purpose for a seminary's existence, namely, toward a better ministry.

At Concordia the nonacademic life of the student is placed to a very high degree into the hands of the students for self-direction in the light of the goals of the seminary, mentioned elsewhere in this volume. Accordingly, through membership in the Students' Association, seminarians participate in the administration of the school and in the supervision of student life. A student senate, elected by the students, helps guide campus activities and service agencies. As a former student body president put it:

> The entire program teaches, among other things, the permanent good which can come from democratic rule and organized self-control. In these activities outside the classroom, students increase their sense of responsibility toward one another, the seminary, and their future calling.

127

All the members and officers of the association and the senate agree on a common goal: to foster a spirit of unity among the students of Concordia Seminary. They constantly learn that a Christian can exercise significant leadership in simple acts of loving service.

The spiritual life committee of the association coordinates the work of the committees dealing with the spiritual growth of the students. The worship committee encourages and implements private and public worship. The stewardship committee promotes Christian stewardship in all areas of living. The world mission council fosters interest in home and foreign missions. Through the "Panta Ta Ethne" program seminarians, by their prayers and offerings, support various mission endeavors of the Synod.

To broaden the general cultural experience of the seminarians, the lyceum committee sponsors choirs, speakers, and a motion picture program; commissions works of art, music, and literature; and sponsors emphasis weeks on art, architecture, music, literature, and drama.

An intramural program, with a full-time director, attracts a very high percentage of the students and teaches them to observe rules of health. The seminary also participates in a limited program of intercollegiate competition in baseball, basketball, tennis, golf, bowling, and track. The fieldhouse and athletic field offer facilities for other sports activities.

In addition to these opportunities to keep physically fit the seminary has a health center, staffed by two consulting physicians, a full-time nurse, and student orderlies. Professional services are available as needed, and annual physical health examinations are provided to train the men to take proper care of themselves on a regular basis. Healthy bodies are essential for the person of the pastor as he meets the rigors of his daily schedule.

Music plays a large part in campus life. Seminarians sing in the Chapel Choir and Schola Cantorum, the Seminary Chorus, the Lutheran Hour Chorus, the Concordia Cantata Chorus, and the chorus of the St. Louis Bach Society. Also on campus are a photography club, radio and TV workshop, speech choir, astronomy club, Greek club, human relations society, and a Lutheran Education Association branch.

Each dormitory unit is under the supervision of a dormitory council and works for good order and harmonious relations within each unit. The leader of this dormitory council is known as the Senator and serves as the elder among his peers. He supervises the dormitory and serves as a willing counselor for any member of his living unit.

It need hardly be stated that in all this living together on the campus the students receive many opportunities to learn the first principles of the Christian ideal set forth by Paul to the Galatians (5:13): "By love serve one another." As men who will need to meet and serve people of all walks of life and all types of anxieties, it is most helpful that they learn to live together under Christ and with every intention of showing love to one another in their daily contacts and pursuits. There is a sort of intimate contagion that takes hold of the men, traditionally called "Men of the Quad," in this rather unique brotherhood. They range in age, generally speaking, from 21 to 26 years, and they come from a variety of backgrounds as well as from different parts of these United States and Canada. As much as feasible their individuality is maintained, but their development as persons takes on a distinctive character to the degree that many a seminarian has been quickly identified for what he is and stands for in the community.

At no small cost to the church the resident program is kept going, and it remains a source of steady concern to the administrative officers and to the teaching staff that the wonderful opportunities for growth individually and as a group are recognized and used to the optimum extent. Here there is little chance that a man as a man can hide limitations and weaknesses of character. They live so closely with one another that they are fairly well known for what they are — men of God, yes, but also sinners in daily need of forgiveness and grace to grow. Here it is that brother can learn to serve brother with the Gospel of forgiveness and to develop these gifts of grace in brotherly admonition which will enhance his person and make it possible for him to meet the many and trying needs of his parishioners. Here it is that the brother learns to use his tongue for the edifying of the body of Christ and to conduct himself in such a manner that he will show that he walks by the Spirit (Gal. 5:16). Here it is where many of the basic skills for working with people are learned for a lifetime of service. Here it is that we seek not simply conformity but that unity in Christ which makes the Lord real to His people and the presence of the Spirit obvious. With a teaching staff also dedicated to attain this goal, it proves to be a privilege to be associated with this brotherhood and a constant challenge to ever greater ability to achieve the principle of Christian living, as alluded to by Paul to the Ephesians: "Rather, speaking the truth in love, we are to grow up in every way into Him who is the Head, into Christ, from whom the whole body, joined and knit together by every joint with which it is supplied, when each part is working properly, makes bodily growth and upbuilds itself in love." (Eph. 5:15, 16 RSV)

Closely allied to this process on the campus the student engages in contact with people off the campus in field work. Classroom lectures and discussions alone cannot prepare a person for today's complex ministry; he must also have practice in preaching, teaching, counseling, and in leading young people.

This practice is supplied through the seminary's field work

program. More than 60 congregations in the St. Louis area welcome students of theology as fellow members. Here, under careful supervision, each seminarian teaches a Sunday school class, teaches a unit of religion in a teaching practicum in one of some 40 Christian day schools, leads Walther League topic discussions, and learns how a congregation operates. Through heart-to-heart discussions with the pastor the seminarian begins to experience the thrill of shepherding God's people.

To acquire special skills for visiting the sick and counseling the aged and infirm, every student does some hospital and institutional work. Often, after his calls, he will write a verbatim account of his visit so that a chaplain-supervisor can help him improve his ministry to the sick and lonely.

None of this training, however, is regarded as mere practice. The seminarian's field experience serves people; he ministers while he learns.

Of particular interest is the volunteer training at Barnes Hospital, where students work as orderlies in a general, then in a mental hospital. Attendance at special lectures by medical doctors and psychiatrists, plus opportunities to serve as student chaplains, helps develop exceptional skills. Many of these volunteers later become chaplains in institutions throughout the world. Most of them will continue their development of these specialized skills by the clinical training program which is also conducted under the guidance of the seminary and associated with accredited clinical training centers.

Full-time work in a parish for 12 months, known as the vicarage, climaxes the seminarian's practical experience. Through deep involvement in the life of the congregation the student vicar learns to apply the Word of God to the life of people. The pastor-supervisor shares his ministry with his young Timothy and through a close father-son relationship passes on to the student the fruits of his own experience.

In recent years the presence of wives of numerous seminarians on the campus has only underscored the importance of their opportunity to work in the Kingdom as the helper of a servant of the Word. It is commonly believed that a pastor's wife can make or break his effectiveness as a minister. Whether we wish to agree with this statement or not, it does remain a fact that a minister's wife wields a great influence on the pastor and on his people. Fortunate is the man who has been blessed by the Lord with a lifemate who can minister to him as a sinner and as a child of God. To assure him by word and life of the Lord's forgiveness in his sometimes terrifying task is her blessed privilege. To know her rightful place by his side as a complement to his person in the work of the Lord is the special grace which comes only from the wholesome and compelling influence of the Holy Spirit. As someone has so aptly put it: "She is not the vice-president in the congregation but the one who has the best opportunity to minister to the minister in his needs."

As we think of the pastor as a person and the importance that is attached to his faith and life, we cannot but conclude by recommending Luther's Sacristy Prayer to all faithful pastors who sense their personal unworthiness to have been called to this blessed task but who also know and love Christ for the opportunities that He grants them as servants of the Word.

Luther's Sacristy Prayer

O Lord God, dear Father in heaven, I am, indeed, unworthy of the office and ministry in which I am to make known Thy glory and to nurture and to serve this congregation.

But since Thou hast appointed me to be a pastor and teacher, and the people are in need of the teachings and the instructions, oh, be Thou my Helper, and let Thy holy angels attend me.

Then if Thou art pleased to accomplish anything through me to Thy glory and not to mine or to the praise of men, grant me, out of Thy pure grace and mercy, a right understanding of Thy Word and that I may also diligently perform it.

O Lord Jesus Christ, Son of the living God, Thou Shepherd and Bishop of our souls, send Thy Holy Spirit that He may work with me, yea, that He may work in me to will and to do through Thy divine strength according to Thy good pleasure. Amen!

NOTES

1. Ewald Plass. *What Luther Says: An Anthology* (St. Louis: Concordia Publishing House, 1959), p. 926.
2. Ross P. Scherer. "Ministers of The Lutheran Church — Missouri Synod: Origins, Training, Career-lines, Perceptions of Work and Reference," unpublished doctoral dissertation (University of Chicago, 1963).
3. Idem, "The Lutheran Ministry: Origins, Careers, Self-Appraisal," *The Cresset*, XXVI (January 1963), 11.
4. Leonhard C. Wuerffel. "A Study of Changes in a Theological Student's Concept of the Ministry During the Year of Internship," unpublished dissertation (St. Louis: Washington University, 1961).
5. Gustav Jensen. *The Ministry*, trans. O. E. Brandt (Minneapolis: Augsburg Publishing House, n. d.), p. 76.
6. Tom Allan. *The Face of My Parish* (New York: Harper, 1953), p. 101.

Worshiping Pastors and Worshiping People

GEORGE W. HOYER

The Threefold Significance of Worship

Every act of worship at a theological seminary has a triple significance.

Of primary significance is the *expressive* aspect of worship, that God, who commanded, "Thou shalt worship" and "Thou shalt serve," *is* served and *is* worshiped. Everything that is included in the broadest sense of "worship" is to be expressed by man's heart and soul, strength and mind. God gives His grace to His church and expects the response of worship. He expects the response that is faith. "Faith is that worship which receives God's offered blessings.... It is by faith that God wants to be worshiped, namely, that we receive from Him what He promises and offers" (Apology IV, 49). He expects the response that focuses in adoration and includes thanksgiving and supplication. God desires, even as does His apostle St. Paul, "that in every place the men should pray, lifting holy hands..." (1 Tim. 2:8). He looks for a corporate response in which the gifts we receive from God are shared with one another even as we join in adoration of the Giver. God expects both our lips and our lives to be expressive of this worship. Through Jesus Christ we are urged not only to "continually offer up a sacrifice of praise to God, that is, the fruit of lips that acknowledge His name," but also "to do good and to share what you have, for such sacrifices are pleasing to God." (Heb. 13:15, 16)

135

A second significance is the fact that every act of worship is also *impressive*. By the very action of adoration or devoted service there is brought to bear upon the worshiper in a very personal way a reflex impact of that love of God which attracts our adoration and draws our devotion. When a Christian remembers to adore, he is reminded of all that is adorable about God, whom he adores. A gift of God has been given to Christian men by pastoral hands in Holy Baptism, and by parental hands which so evidently served in love that these men have seen their good works and glorify the Father in heaven. That gift of God which is in them by *that* kind of laying on of hands is stirred up within themselves by the folding of their own hands. When men are involved in their worship action toward God, they experience the action of God toward them. The divine power is as surely operative in this impressive way while man acts in worship as it is when God acts initially or responds to the prayer that depends on His promises. It is within the action of man's response that the means of grace most effectively release their power. Obviously, it is when the Lord's Supper is *celebrated,* when the liturgy is *done,* that the blessings of Body and Blood can be received. But equally true is it that when the worshiper expresses in his own words of devotion the revealed truths that he knows of God, they reach him most specifically, spoken by his own tongue. When he says "God" to God, he also says "God" to himself. Every act of adoration, confession, thanksgiving and supplication is also a work of proclamation to the one who worships. This impressive reflex makes an act of worship itself a *means* of the means of grace.

A third significant aspect of seminary worship is its *cumulative effect*. The worship life of seminarians becomes the worship life of pastors, and the worship life of pastors touches the lives of the worshipers in congregations. *That* congregational worship in thousands of parishes is both expressive and impressive. *That* parish worship expresses the result of the action of God that makes men Christian and that calls men into the ministry. But that parish worship also contains a reflex impact of the power of God that stirs up the Spirit's gifts and sends men to seminaries. In seminaries men worship — and the triple significance of their worship of the Triune God must again be reckoned with. Their worship life has already been conditioned to a great extent in both form and content by the parish worship life of which they have been a part. Much that they bring with them to the common worship life of their school is uncommon — Spirit-given, Spirit-shaped; but much is of very prosaic origin — grounded on "in our church at home we . . ."; conceived in terms of "at home my parents . . ."; and limited by "my pastor never does . . ." or "our teachers never explained. . . ." Without presuming to judge how their expressions of worship impress God, it is apparent, and it is inevitable, that the quality of their worship will make its impression both on their own selves and on the fellow students with whom they have such repeated corporate experiences in receiving the grace of God and in responding to it. Continuation in less than worthy practices of worship may actually be teaching and reteaching the false theological and devotional ideas on which these practices are actually, though unconsciously, based. That kind of teaching is likely to be most successful and most sinister because of its learn-by-doing technique and its implicit acceptance of premises which never become apparent and which operate in a deeper level than that of the mind. The concern that is felt over any student body *conduct* that contradicts Christian conviction is surely justified, for when men fail to do the everyday things of life to the glory of God, they are living a lie and undermining, if not forsaking, their faith. At least as large a concern ought to be felt toward the conduct of *worship* in a student body. The fact that what is taken for granted is often more efficiently communicated than what is more obviously expressed in words ought to be a warning that less than worthy *worship* practices can be corrosive of both faith and life in our seminaries.

The part that "a more excellent ministry" will play in this continually recurring cycle of worshiping is obvious. The more worthily the minister worships, the more effectively he will teach worship to the worshiping parishioners by example and instruction. The more worthily the parish worships, the more its individual worshipers will be affected by worship's reflex action. The more effective this impressive action is in the lives of students who go to the church's seminaries, the more worthy the worshiping life of the school and of the ministers it graduates.

The importance of the practice of worship at our seminaries in the shaping of that "more excellent ministry" should also be obvious. Unless the seminaries are able to exert a strongly significant influence in the midst of the expressive, impressive, and cumulative aspects of student worship, much of their hope for a more excellent ministry in the coming years is likely to be thwarted. It is obvious that worship practices will continue to reduplicate themselves, and wherever there are unworthy practices, they will simply multiply the problems instead of magnifying God. It is then apparent that the premises and practices which a seminary adopts in order to carry its cooperative share with the Spirit in training worshiping pastors is a vital part of the school's curriculum. Unanimous agreement on the worship premises and practices to be adopted at its seminaries by an American Lutheran synod such as ours will not be automatic or easy. A church denomination which over the years has been given its worship habits and preferences within the circuit of these threefold worship forces, affected by the cultural, the linguistic, the nationalistic factors of its history, and without such a strongly directed influence as it is here envisioned from its seminaries, could not be expected to emerge with a common understanding of the way of worship to be fostered. Decisions as to the practices of seminary worship must be made in a serious awareness of the crucial importance of the devotional life and at the same time with a vital sense both of the catholicity of Lutheranism and of its Reformation heritage.

The Fourfold Action of Worship

Such a rapid summary of the significance of worship makes it apparent that the broad term "worship" must be analyzed and understood if its place in the training of a more excellent ministry is to be utilized either by those who plan the course of learning or by those who undertake it.

It is certainly true that Christian worship is the work of God. This is the basic theological assertion that must be the foundation of any consideration of worship, of any instruction in worship, and of all acts of worship. It is God who *makes* men both to will and to do, but as men of God *they worship*. Every man in Christ is a new creature, and worship is the work of new men.

If seminarians can be helped through instruction in the fundamental realization that they must *act* in all phases and aspects of worship; if they can be helped to understand the methodology of worship and thereby grow in the grace of worship and the skills of worshiping, they will be equipped to assist the members of their parishes to become more devoted worshipers. This, then, is a first and a fundamental part of the seminaries' significant influence on worshiping pastors and worshiping people.

The fourfold action of worship is a basic frame for the understanding of seminarians who worship and for graduates who undertake the instruction task with parishes.

Man must catch the impetus of the Word of God. Before the Word became incarnate the Virgin Mary must say, "Let it be to me according to your word" (Luke 1:38). No *such* overshadowing by the Holy Ghost is offered to the worshiper in today's pew, but this same kind of anticipation ought to be in every worshiper's mind. If the hope of gaining a double portion of the Spirit in the temple of our bodies is what is meant when we settle back hoping "to get something out of" the service, the lessons, and the sermon, then it is a worthy worship attitude. But if there is instead an implicit challenge to another *man* to supply something in the way of interesting information and knowledge, then we have missed the first requirement of action in worship, that we be ready to catch the Word. A church that has been commanded to go out and disciple by the Word in words and water must itself be made up of men, women, and children who continuously depend on the grace God gave in the water of Holy Baptism and who deliberately set themselves to catch the Word God gives through the Sacred Scriptures. Nor is the responsibility of each man to catch the working Word of God anywhere made more explicit than in our Lord's words at the institution of the Holy Communion, "This do." The new men take and eat the Lord's body; they take and all drink of the Lord's blood. And in that "catching" action, in the "remembering," the Lord's work is made a present reality for them, for their forgiveness, life, and salvation.

Obviously an awareness of this vital first responsibility of the worshiper must also be dominant in the intention of those who speak the Word from chancel and from pulpit. The liturgist is to help men "do their liturgy," their reasonable common service. He cannot neglect conveying information, and he desires to make sense; but primarily he wants to create a channel for worship out of the chancel phrases he speaks. The sermon gives God a 20th-century vocabulary to bring the power of the Word into the heart of today's man. But the sermon in its place in worship must be purposeful as well as pertinent. It must seek to move hearers to worship God at this time in this service, so that they will have taken the first step in the *life* of service to God and man. The sermon dare not be the sound of man pontificating but must always convey the sense of the church at work edifying itself in love. And the sermon's heart must always be the heart of God, whose love alone creates forgiven worshipers. All this must be realized by those who structure courses in liturgics and homiletics and by those who arrange the services of worship. Men who are so assisted from within and from without to take in the Word will know the power of the Highest overshadowing them in their worship. The holy thing that is born in this action of worship is still the Son of God, Christ in us, the Hope of glory.

Man must give a response to God, who speaks and acts for him. This is the second of the fourfold actions in worship. So great is the priority of God that men ought to give Him glory and praise even if He had done nothing for man. Man could not, of course, love God if God had not first loved him. But, thanks be to God, He has — which increases the necessity of man's response. Nothing should be allowed to obscure the basic responsibility of man to adore God.

Even this brief a reminder of God's majesty makes evident man's continual necessity to confess his own creatureliness and sinful rebelliousness to the Holy One. "If we confess our sins, He is faithful and just and will forgive our sins and cleanse us from all unrighteousness" (1 John 1:9). Once again everything has been done by God. Nothing remains for man to do. And yet this action must be *done* by man, or nothing of the everything is his own.

In the knowledge of all that God is, and has done, and is doing continuously, no man can fail to give thanks to the Lord. He is good. Call no man good but God; but call God good! Man must be the one who gives thanks. What shall we render to the

Lord for all His goodness? This at least, this as the first gift, which implies the gift of all of life — thanksgiving.

God's gift of the privilege of prayer makes clear again man's responsibility to *do.* Man's supplications and intercessions are both his joy and his obedience. And even here, where the objective seems to be the receiving of answers and of aid, the actual substance of Christian prayer is adoration. "Thy will be done" involves submission, but basically it is adoration.

Chapel programs that are arranged to meet the first requirement of worship, the catching of the Word, are not likely to err in this second aspect of worship's action. They are structured in an awareness that worship by basic definition is giving God the glory due His name. But confusion in the purpose of the liturgical proclamation of the Word and removal of the primary note of adoration as the response of new men to the Word go hand in hand. It must be made clear in seminary and in parish that worshipers who do not come to adore change even the most powerful proclamation into another course of classroom instruction. On the other hand, those who deliberately kneel, as new men are able to do, in joyful adoration, are already saying, "Be it unto me according to Thy Word" and are ready to catch the power. Whenever worship is structured within the stance of praise, the best climate has been created for the reception of, as well as the response to, the working Word of God.

Nor can the new man lose sight of the fact that Christian worship is done by *men* of God. *Man must share with his fellowman in the Word and work of worship.* All Christian men are to let the Word of Christ dwell in them richly by teaching and admonishing one another in all wisdom and by singing psalms and hymns and spiritual songs with thankfulness in their hearts to God (Col. 3:16). The God of all comfort comforts the new men so that they may comfort others (2 Cor. 1:4). The new men

142

rejoice together in the remembrance that by one Spirit they were baptized into one body (1 Cor. 12:13). And the verbs of command in the Eucharist's instructions are all in the plural, just because the church is *one*. In worship, certainly, new men bear one another's burdens even while each bears his own. Each man must catch, each man must give, but each man must also share both in the catching and the giving.

This fact of brotherhood is partly a matter of information. But it is not a *knowledge* of relationship that makes a family a family. Family life must be lived. In the church, too, blood is thicker than water — is it fair to make a play on these words and suggest that here is one of the reasons why our Lord instituted the sacrament of His body and His blood, to complement our adoption by Holy Baptism's water? The cup of blessing is a participation in the blood of Christ; and the bread is a participation in the body of Christ. "Because there is one loaf, we who are many are one body, for we all partake of the same loaf" (1 Cor. 10:15-17). Can parish or student body ever do better in its attempt to realize its oneness than to take up the offer of its Head to experience its unity in Him and in one another? It is difficult in the very nature of an assembly of worshipers to express in words the unity that is basic to the responsibility of sharing; but when the unity is experienced, when the experience is realized "often," then a look will be the words, and the very presence of the body a realization of the action of sharing.

Worship as new men's work is not complete until it is crystallized as living. *Man must live his worship toward the fellowship and toward the world.* St. Paul appeals by the mercies of God to new men to present their bodies "as a living sacrifice" and defines such service as "spiritual worship" (Rom. 12:1). It is obvious again that what is required here is man's action in response to the appeal and the action of God. It is what the new man does, in word and deed, that is to be in the name of the Lord Jesus and thereby become worship.

Since the living of worship toward those in the fellowship of the redeemed is an aspect of "sharing," the accent here should be on action toward those in the world who are redeemed and do not know it. The mission of the church must be a steady descant to all worship in the church. Opportunities for the mission, which is life as worship, must be supplied in the day-to-day life of the seminary or the parish community. A seminary's program of field work and a required year of vicarage provide vital areas for worship to be lived.

The Fivefold Frame of Reverence for the Worship Action

This fourfold action of worship must be learned and taught for the development of "a more excellent ministry." But so significant is the impressive aspect of worship, and so central is the action of response to the realization of worship's values, and so necessary in our day is the accent on worship as a work for God's man to do, that concerned attention must be given to details by which the worship response is stimulated.

Fundamental to all of this, of course, is the fact that students are the church and need the Word of God. Continuously the Word in water must be recalled, the Word in print be read, the Word in speech be said, the Word in bread and wine be received, the Word in worship be expressed, the Word in life be shared. In all this the student body is being the body. The students become more aware of — they become the more — the church. Wherever else the church is, it is on the seminary campus. However else the church lives its life, a central manifestation is in its corporate worship. If the awareness of the church is to be fostered, the place of worship in the body's life should be visualized before anything else is scheduled, as everything else in the curriculum and in extracurricular areas is structured. The importance we give to the church is often both seen and given by the position granted to worship in the midst of other aspects of campus life.

Men of the campus are not men of the world, but are men in the world. Since their lives are lived in a world whose frame of reference is the worship of things, they need a frame of *reverence* to hold them to the worship of the one true God. There is but a fine verbal line between "in" and "of" the world. Firm, solid lines must be drawn if the distinction is to be preserved in living. Five lines are here drawn to suggest the kind of worship life that would serve as the mold for a worthy expression of worship, would significantly affect worship's cumulative effect on the church's ministry, and would make its impression on the new man in the men of the student body.

Men still centered in self need the catholicity of the church's liturgy. For corporate action there must be liturgy. That liturgy should certainly be the expression of the group that is worshiping; but it ought also express the historic and contemporary reality of the church of which the group is a part. Not only should God speak and we speak, but the voices of the innumerable company of saints and angels should be heard as well. When the company on the farther shore and in the greater light converse with us, it is easier for us to speak with one another and for us to see one another as what we indeed are, the members of the body of which our Lord is the Head. If practical application extends along this line, it will require the kind of regeneration only the Spirit works in the liturgical practices of some of the congregations that surround seminaries, or the serious consideration of campus congregations in which students hold membership supplementary to their membership in parishes elsewhere in the city.

145

Children of creation must worship with created things.
Pervading the whole area of worship is the unavoidable complication of humanity itself. Men and angels worship, but the men who matriculate at seminaries are not angels, and it is these men in their humanity who must be helped to worship. Man was not designed to get away from himself, and so man's physical design ought to be utilized in order to help him "come to himself" and return to the Father's house. If worship is to be expressed to the Creator, and is to have its impressive results on the creature, ceremony, symbol, and the sound of music must make visual, audible, and sensible the realness of God, who is Spirit. If a recognized obligation to the synod which supports the schools is the motive for a certain number of hours of chore work by students on certain campuses, would not the obligations of the creature to the Creator provide sufficient prompting for hours of worship's chores undertaken by every student either individually or in the choir of his dormitory? The making of a joyful noise is not so much the task of selected voices as of chosen people.

Men of small vision need a place in which to see God.
God deigns to dwell in houses made with hands. A seminary surely should take Him up on His goodness and prepare a place dedicated to His name alone. It was in a temple vision that Isaiah saw the King, the Lord of Hosts. It was there he knew his guilt removed, his sin forgiven. It was there he heard God say, "Whom shall I send, and who will go for us?" It was there and then he said, "Here am I! Send me."

People of our times need the year of the church. God, who came in the fullness of time, ought not be crowded out by godless times. The difference between being the church in our time and simply a church marking time is partly the difference between living the liturgical year and preserving the year as a curio. One way to make sure we realize that our times are in His hands is to let Him place His hands on our time. It is difficult to snatch some time for God out of a busy schedule, but once the whole year has been given over to God, He always supplies enough time for us to work while it is day. And the year is a matter of days, all the days of the week lived out in the frame of the Lord's Days. The living out is a matter of the lessons, of all the propers being utilized, of Sundays celebrated all week. Once the church year is seriously lived on a seminary campus, its values of acted Gospel will strengthen men to live their lives for God.

Men who live with the children of darkness are helped by the daily offices. Here Lutheran catholicity and Lutheran Reformation heritage are wedded. The daily use of matins and vespers on a seminary campus will help to make both real. In their daily use much of the necessity of man's action, of the priority of adoration in worship becomes evident, and many of the values of the church's liturgy and the church's year are focused. Those who worship within their discipline are given a useful tool for dedicating each day to God.

It ought to be noted that these items are not expressions of a fervent hope, but areas of present development in the worship life at Concordia Seminary. The goal of a more excellent ministry, a worthily worshiping ministry, is being approached not only by efforts on this campus but by the schools who prepare for enrollment at this seminary, including the parishes and the parish schools from which the students come.

There is an increasing awareness of the importance of worship at Concordia Seminary. There is recognition of the fact that every instructor, every administrative officer, is concerned with the Christian life of the students, including their worship life; but this has not crowded out the understanding that an area as technically specialized and as vitally important as the worship men

147

offer in the presence of God and in the house of God ought to be the concern and care of a man appointed to that work. The coming years of training a more excellent ministry should see the priority of worship affecting everything in our school, its calendar and schedule, its catalogs and courses, and, pray God, always its faculty and especially its students. Worshiping students now, they will be worshiping pastors, worshiping with people.

Why Go into Something Else?

MARTIN H. SCHARLEMANN

Seminary Devotion, April 29, 1963
(On the Monday after Misericordias Domini)

The shadow of the cross keeps lingering; it refuses to fade. Here we are, just beyond the Second Sunday After Easter, and once again the Epistle for the day is back at words about our suffering Savior. The last verse of the lesson reads: "By His wounds you have been healed. For you were straying like sheep, but have now been turned to the Shepherd and Guardian of your souls." (1 Peter 2:25)

We are fortunate that the Cross persists, for it is a source of healing. It is a creative event, offering us a focus, a future, and a profession.

"You have been healed, for you were straying," says the apostle. Man's malady is that of wandering off on his own, asserting his independence. Man insists on his freedom, and some-times God grants the request. He burdens man with his autonomy, and then life becomes meaningless. Under such circumstances, to quote *South Pacific,* the individual feels "stuck like a dope with a thing called hope," for life is out of focus.

The frustration and emptiness of modern life has rarely been put more eloquently than by T. S. Eliot in a few lines that he calls "An Epitaph to Suburbia." Here they are:

Here lived a decent, godless people;
Their only monument the asphalt road and a thousand
lost golf balls.

151

From this kind of futility we have been healed, says the apostle. We have been turned, all of us, to the Shepherd and Guardian of our souls. This creates a sense of community, of belonging. Out of sheep we have been made into a flock, with a Shepherd, whose task it is to lead us and so open up for us the avenue to a God-centered life. In the Scripture lesson chosen for today (Ezek. 34:11-16) Ezekiel calls this a gathering of the sheep. Each one is turned around, so to speak, to face the Shepherd, and that provides a focus for all of us jointly.

The Cross also offers us a future. Let us remember that in the temple at Jerusalem sacrifices were occasions for joy. Sacrificing consisted of a rite by which a person liquidated his past and received new life. The individual who brought a sacrifice identified himself with the victim; as the animal died all of that man's past ugliness, shoddiness, all of his sins, were removed.

We, however, did not bring the sacrifice of Christ Jesus; the Father did. But in Baptism He arranged to have us identified with the victim. And so our past is liquidated at the Cross. Our solidarity with Adam died there; for we are buried with Christ by Baptism into death that even as He rose from the dead we should walk in newness of life. The future opens up before us. Our Shepherd is up front, leading us, calling us to see and hear Him. Such a forward pull, incidentally, is characteristic of all Biblical revelation. It keeps pointing us to the promises of God, whose fulfillment lies in the future — even as we now await our Shepherd's return.

The Cross also provides healing by giving us a profession. The word *shepherd* means "pastor." In Eph. 4, pastors are ranged with apostles, prophets, evangelists, and teachers as gifts of the risen Lord to His church. He Himself is called our Master Shepherd, as a matter of fact. He trains us, so to speak, through institutions like this seminary of ours, to lead as shepherds, so that men might hear and live. You will discover as you go into this profession that you yourself will find healing in the process of losing your life to find it.

Some weeks ago a mission secretary of one of our larger Districts did a study of the pastors of his particular region in terms of their general attitude and outlook. He was saddened to discover that many of them seem to think of the parish ministry as a place to prepare for going somewhere else. To him and to us this is rather disturbing news. Why should this be? Why should a pastor want to go into something else?

We train you here as persons equipped to serve as the guardians of life's crises. Parents with a broken heart, having lost their only son, will entrust their spiritual life to you as their pastor, looking to you and listening to find in your limping words comfort and strength as they focus on the Cross and beyond that on God's open future. Again, we instruct you in such things as administering the Sacrament of Baptism, where something so exciting and mysterious goes on that, as the apostle reminds us (1 Peter 1:12), angels are anxious to get some small glimpse into all that God accomplishes there.

You will have the privilege of taking people into classes of adult instruction, and there you will note how even their faces change as their life takes on meaning and focus — especially about the time you get to a discussion of the Third Article!

You are taught here to be the kind of shepherd who will lead his people as they join "with angels and archangels and all the company of heaven" in lauding and magnifying God's glorious name. The veil between time and eternity becomes very thin at this moment, believe me.

Now, where else do you have such undeserved privileges? Why go into something else? Why indeed?

153